Jardineras y balconeras

H. P. HAAS

*Cómo diseñar y cuidar
fácilmente tu jardín*

HISPANO EUROPEA

índice

Directora de la colección: **Carme Farré Arana.**

Título de la edición original: **Balkonkästen.**

Es propiedad, BLV
© 2002 BLV Verlagsgesellschaft
mbH, München

© de la traducción: Fernando Ruiz Gabás.

© de la edición en castellano, 2006:
Editorial Hispano Europea, S. A.
Primer de Maig, 21 - Pol. Ind. Gran Via Sud
08908 L'Hospitalet - Barcelona, España.
E-mail: hispanoeuropea@hispanoeuropea.com
Web: www.hispanoeuropea.com

Depósito Legal: B. 21313-2006.

ISBN: 84-255-1663-3.

IMPRESO EN ESPAÑA   PRINTED IN SPAIN

LIMPERGRAF, S. L. - Mogoda, 29-31 (Pol. Ind. Can Salvatella)
08210 Barberà del Vallès

Un balcón de ensueño

La multitud de formas y de colores de las flores permite crear composiciones magníficas.

Déjate encantar con la belleza de la naturaleza, las flores, sus perfumes y sus colores. Este manual es una fuente de continua inspiración: siguiendo sus ideas podrás realizar magníficas balconeras para aprovechar plenamente el esplendor del verano.

En esta guía descubrirás numerosas composiciones floridas. Para conseguirlas, no es necesario ser un jardinero extraordinario. ¡Incluso los principiantes pueden intentar esta aventura! Indicamos aquí las plantas recomendadas, pero no es obligatorio utilizarlas todas y, partiendo de nuestros consejos, se puede realizar una creación personal. Al final del volumen incluimos una pequeña guía práctica con indicaciones técnicas de utilidad y también podrás encontrar las fotografías de todas las plantas mencionadas. En total, hemos seleccionado 54 especies de calidad. Combinándolas, se consigue una sorprendente variedad de composiciones.

Larga experiencia

Todas las asociaciones de plantas que se proponen en este manual ya han sido comprobadas y funcionan muy bien. Cuando insistimos en una variedad determinada de planta (por ej., el geranio «Gran Prix»), se debe frecuentemente a que sólo esta variedad presenta la característica deseada. Por el contrario, allí donde las variedades son intercambiables, solamente se menciona el color preferido y las variedades utilizadas se citan meramente a título de ejemplo.

Casi todas las combinaciones son posibles, aunque, por supuesto, ¡contra gustos y colores no hay disputas!

Sin embargo, los profesionales se inclinan frecuentemente por la teoría del color. Algunos optan por una combinación triple, reuniendo tres colores vivos que armonizan bien unos con otros. En cambio, otros prefieren los colores complementarios que se refuerzan entre sí (el amarillo y el violeta, por ejemplo). También se busca el contraste entre tonos fríos y tonos cálidos, o se recurre a degradados de colores para dar un toque muy personal a la balconera.

La mayoría de composiciones que aquí se proponen deben colocarse a pleno sol o a media sombra. Se presentan diversas combinaciones de colores. Pero también hemos pensado en los balcones con sombra, en los amantes de los perfumes y en los gastrónomos. Todas las composiciones se han hecho para jardineras anchas (20 cm), en las cuales la plantación tiene lugar en dos filas. Por otra parte, puede observarse que existen diferentes tipos de plantas. Las plantas dominantes constituyen la estructura básica de la composición. Las plantas de relleno realzan el valor de las anteriores y permiten variar los conjuntos. De este modo, y con medios muy sencillos, tu balcón puede transformarse en un verdadero oasis de verdor. ¡Sólo de ti depende conseguir este lugar de calma y de descanso que respira vitalidad!

La combinación ingeniosa de plantas dominantes y de relleno permite crear continuamente nuevas composiciones florales.

Balcón clásico en rojo y amarillo

La planta de balcón más corriente, y también la más fácil de cultivar, es, y seguirá siendo, sin duda, el geranio. Es muy apreciada en las zonas rurales, donde adorna balcones y terrazas. Esta vivaz parece preferir particularmente los balcones de las viviendas y las granjas de las montañas. Visibles desde lejos, las fachadas floridas rivalizan en belleza para despertar la admiración de los paseantes, y forman paisajes de verdaderas tarjetas postales. También es habitual en los balcones de los pueblos andaluces y del litoral mediterráneo. Por tanto, no es sorprendente que muchos amantes de las flores vuelvan siempre a esta clásica.
En efecto, el geranio ofrece colores de luminosidad sin igual, y una floración abundante y duradera a la vez. Frecuentemente se le mezcla con otras flores, a pesar de que ya sea muy imponente. Hemos escogido un rojo luminoso que puedes asociar con flores blancas, azules o amarillas, según tu gusto. Hemos optado por el bidens amarillo.

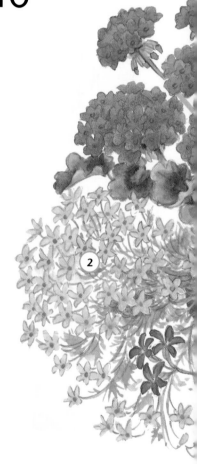

Lo que necesitas aquí

1 Geranio zonal *(Pelargonium × hortorum)*, «Grand Prix», rojo luminoso: × 4

2 Bidens, verbena amarilla *(Bidens ferulifolia)*, «Compact», amarillo: × 2

3 Gitanillas, geranio de hiedra *(Pelargonium peltatum)*, «Leucht-Cascade», rojo luminoso: × 1

Cómo plantar

Hemos limitado el número de plantas en esta maceta conscientemente. En efecto, las tres flores escogidas son exigentes y de naturaleza dominante, y necesitan mucho espacio. Esta composición se desarrollará rápidamente en el curso del verano y no tardarás en comprender que el pequeño número de plantas era más que suficiente.

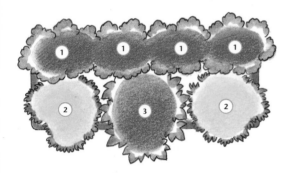

Plano de la composición de página 7, maceta de 80 × 20 cm

Así pues, detrás plantarás cuatro matas de geranio zonal. Delante, colocarás un geranio de hiedra, y a derecha e izquierda de este último, dos bidens. Si consideras que hay poco geranio hiedra, puedes invertir las plantas, instalando entonces en primera fila un bidens rodeado de dos geranios hiedra.

La plantación ha de efectuarse al tresbolillo, es decir las filas están desniveladas entre sí. Por otra parte, hay que procurar comprar variedades buenas. En el caso de los geranios zonales, están de moda las variedades de hojas oscuras. Estas nuevas generaciones han mejorado de aspecto y son muy bellas. Sin embargo, son muy compactas, y por tanto no producen necesariamente el mejor efecto en la balconera. Por tal razón hemos optado por una variedad de geranio más alta. Para el geranio de hiedra, recomendamos encarecidamente las variedades antiguas en cascada, con flores sencillas que tienen la ventaja de ser muy robustas y de ofrecer una floración abundante.

En cuanto al bidens, los cruces han conseguido frenar de manera significativa el crecimiento loco de las variedades antiguas, que tenían tendencia a la invasión salvaje. Las plantas formarán matas por cada lado de la maceta, y desde allí empezarán rápidamente a colgar bellas cascadas de flores.

Cómo cuidar tus plantas

Aquí puede observarse la capacidad invasora del bidens. Incluso los geranios tienen dificultades para hacerse respetar.

Los geranios forman parte de las plantas de balcón que necesitan muy poco mantenimiento. Son ideales para todos aquellos que disponen de poco tiempo. Desde mediados de primavera hasta otoño, florecen sin interrupción y sin fatigarse. Su mejor comportamiento es bajo el sol. Si los colocas a media sombra, la floración será menos abundante a partir del final del verano, hasta que llega un momento en que la planta solamente produce hojas. Además, es aconsejable proteger del viento y de la lluvia a las variedades erguidas y de flores dobles, a fin de evitar que los tallos cedan bajo el peso de las flores. Los tejados salientes de las casas de campo ofrecen así una protección ideal, lo cual explica su bella apariencia.

Aunque los geranios soportan bien una relativa sequía, será necesario prestar atención a que el mantillo permanezca suficientemente húmedo y rico en sustancias nutritivas. Cuando un geranio no está bien nutrido, florece menos, y después sus hojas adquieren un to-no amarillo claro. Por tanto, aconsejamos abonar tu maceta cada semana. Por otra parte, las lluvias demasiado prolongadas pueden causar la podredumbre de las flores y de las hojas. Por consiguiente, limpia tus plantas de vez en cuando. Los geranios de hiedra, de flores simples, se limpian solos, y los pétalos de las flores marchitas caen al suelo, sin necesidad de intervención personal. Los bidens también se mantienen solos, en la medida en que las flores marchitas quedan recubiertas por las flores nuevas. Así pues, la planta se presenta siempre bajo su mejor aspecto. Soporta tanto el viento como la lluvia, pero reacciona bastante mal en caso de sequedad prolongada.

Otras sugerencias

Puedes reemplazar:

(2) por Petunia Surfinia *(Petunia × atkinsiana)* «Sky Blue», azul: × 1

Sol en tu balcón

El amarillo y el naranja son colores que simbolizan el verano, el sol y el calor. Si tienes un balcón orientado al sur, bien expuesto, ésta es tu composición ideal. La combinación de plantas que se propone ofrece colores cálidos que no dejarán de transmitir vida y alegría a quienes la contemplen.

Las flores se abren bajo los rayos del sol

Hemos escogido expresamente plantas que únicamente, o sobre todo, florecen a pleno sol. Así, las flores de la gazania y las de la dimorfoteca solamente desvelan su belleza bajo el calor de los rayos solares. En tiempo de lluvia, por la noche, o en caso de que las flores estén a la sombra, sus botones se cierran para volverse a abrir en una ocasión próxima y mostrar entonces sus brillantes colores.

Lo que necesitas aquí

1. Margarita arbustiva *(Argyranthemum frutescens)*, «Butterfly», amarillo: × 1
2. Zinia *(Zinnia angustifolia)*, «Classic», naranja: × 2

3) **Dimorfoteca** *(Osteospermum ecklonis)*, «Orange Symphonie», naranja: × 2

4) **Estrellada de mar** *(Asteriscus maritimus)*, «Gold Dollar» amarillo: × 2

5) **Gazania** *(Gazania rigens)*, «Czardas Orange», naranja: × 2

6) **Petunia** *(Petunia × atkinsiana)*, «Million Bells Lemon», amarillo: × 1

Cómo plantar

La disposición de las seis plantas es perfectamente simétrica. Las especies más altas se instalan en segundo plano, mientras que las más pequeñas –o sea las plantas colgantes– se colocan delante para que resalten.

La planta dominante situada detrás es, sin duda alguna, la margarita arbustiva amarilla. La variedad «Butterfly» es una de

Plano de la composición de página 11,
maceta de 100 × 20 cm.

sin descanso hasta las primeras heladas. Las dimorfotecas, situadas en los extremos de la fila posterior, utilizarán todo el espacio que se les conceda y delimitarán la composición. La serie «Symphony» presenta notables variedades nuevas que florecen sin cesar a lo largo de todo el verano.

En el centro de la primera fila se plantan las petunias de flores pequeñas. A medida que pase el verano, se transformará en una verdadera planta colgante. La variedad «Million Bells Lemon» que hemos escogido, forma un pequeño matorral típico, que florece incluso en tiempo desapacible, a diferencia de otras numerosas variedades similares.

Por el contrario, la gazania necesita estar a pleno sol para abrir completamente sus flores, las cuales presentan, en compensación, colores de gran intensidad.

La estrellada de mar, con sus flores amarillas y su follaje espeso, se coloca en primera fila por su escasa altura, y necesita sol.

las mejores de color amarillo que se puede encontrar actualmente en el mercado. A derecha e izquierda se desarrollarán las zinias. Sus flores simples de color naranja resisten de modo sorprendente a la lluvia, y se abren

CONSEJO

El riego automático, o la utilización de una maceta con reserva de agua, permite suministrar agua y abono a las plantas mucho más fácilmente.

Cómo cuidar tus plantas

Las flores amarillas y naranja de las petunias «Million Bells» y de la zinia armonizan perfectamente con el tono azulado de la lobelia.

Cuando el balcón está soleado, lo más importante es regar las plantas. Un mantillo demasiado seco o demasiado húmedo provoca una coloración amarillenta de las hojas (clorosis), una suspensión del crecimiento y, en los casos más graves, la muerte del vegetal. Puede ser necesario regar regularmente, a menudo dos veces al día, para responder a las necesidades efectivas de las plantas. En los días más cálidos hay que prever hasta diez litros por metro de balcón, ya que es difícil humidificar de nuevo un mantillo desecado. Así pues, se recomienda mantener la humedad de tus plantas a un nivel regular.

El mantenimiento de las plantas de la familia de las compuestas –tales como las de la mayoría que se emplean aquí (margarita arbustiva, zinia, dimorfoteca, estrellada de mar y gazania)– consiste principalmente en cortar las flores marchitas. Esto impide la producción de semillas y favorece el nacimiento de nuevos botones y el estímulo de la floración. Lamentablemente las margaritas arbustivas amarillas tienen tendencia a atraer a las orugas minadoras. Entonces sus hojas quedan marcadas por los estragos de estos insectos (desgarrones, galerías oscuras que se desecan poco a poco) y cuya visión pronto se vuelve desagradable. Para combatir este problema, se puede recurrir a los insecticidas (a la venta en los establecimientos especializados). Sigue al pie de la letra las instrucciones indicadas en el producto.

Cuando las petunias presentan hojas amarillentas (cloróticas) es señal de que su mantillo está demasiado húmedo o que les falta hierro. Para prevenir el problema, es aconsejable mezclar con el mantillo un abono especial, rico en hierro. Si solamente hay un plano afectado, se debe aportar hierro de manera seleccionada. Procura que el pH de la maceta no sobrepase el 6,5, pues ello suprimiría importantes sustancias nutritivas (tales como el hierro). Si suministras regularmente abono acidificante y el agua necesaria a tus plantas, no tendrás problema alguno.

Composición original en amarillo y rojo

Si te gustan las cosas diferentes, y llevar a cabo nuevas experiencias, este capítulo te interesará. Presenta una balconera que no es como las otras, y que no podrías comprar ya hecha en el florista. Es original, y se la podría calificar como maceta prototipo de última generación.

Plantas trepadoras en maceta

Es probable que los principiantes no conozcan la mayoría de las especies a las que hemos recurrido, pero quizá también se sorprendan algunos jardineros expertos. Así la utilización en maceta de una planta trepadora –dirigida hacia arriba o en cualquier otra dirección– no dejará de asombrarles. Algunos quizá puedan tener la tentación de clamar al cielo, pero sabremos responder a sus críticas. Aunque todavía sea raro encontrar este tipo de novedades en los balcones, no por ello son menos interesantes. Por otra parte, no exigen muchos más cuidados, y su mantenimiento es sencillo, aunque no se sea un experto.

Lo que necesitas aquí

1. Calceolaria *(Calceolaria integrifolia)* «Brigrar Elite», amarilla: × 2
2. Susana de los ojos negros *(Thunbergia alata)*, amarilla: × 1

③ Tabaco ornamental (Nicotiana × sanderae),
«Tuxedo red», roja: × 2

④ Capuchina *(Tropaeolum majus)*,
«Red Wonder», roja: × 1

⑤ Onagra *(Oenothera fruticosa)*,
«African Queen», amarilla: × 2

⑥ Cufea *(Cuphea llavea)*, «Torpedo», roja con corazón
azul oscuro: × 1

⑦ *Alonsoa meridionalis*, «Fireball», naranja: × 1

Cómo plantar

No siempre está clara la instalación de una planta trepadora en maceta, pero la Susana de los ojos negros se adapta perfectamente a nuestra composición. Si deseas verla trepar hacia arriba, necesitarás una escala sencilla constituida por tallos de mimbre o de bambú.

Plano de la composición de página 15, maceta de 120 × 20 cm

A derecha e izquierda de la planta trepadora, hemos instalado las luminosas flores rojas del tabaco ornamental. Al comprarla, se ha de procurar escoger una especie compacta, que no suba más de 50 cm.

En los extremos de la maceta se plantan las calceolarias amarillas. La variedad «Brigrar Elite» es la que se adapta mejor. Tam-

bién puedes optar por «Goldari» o «Goldbukett».

En medio de la primera fila se coloca la cufea, planta nueva de flores en parte tubulares, y que presentan dos grandes pétalos con corola ensanchada, lo cual hace que parezcan cabecitas de Mickey. Al lado, a plena luz, hemos colocado las flores de color amarillo limón de las onagras, otra novedad de las jardinerías. Hay que plantarlas al borde de la maceta, de modo que cuelguen bellamente.

La capuchina «Red Wonder» es la última curiosidad de tu composición. Desde la primera mirada, fascina la luminosidad de sus pétalos color rojo sangre resaltando sobre su follaje verde oscuro. La Alonsoa «Fireball» presenta un porte completamente diferente, pero no menos bello: esta planta delicada y seductora desarrolla innumerables flores de color rojo anaranjado.

CONSEJO

Se pueden podar ligeramente la Alonsoa y el tabaco después de su floración para favorecer el nacimiento de nuevos botones y la recuperación de la floración.

Cómo cuidar tus plantas

La Susana de los ojos negros necesita un emplazamiento luminoso y protegido del viento. Si le suministras regularmente agua y abono, crecerá sin dificultades. Se recomienda dirigir los nuevos brotes en la dirección deseada de vez en cuando. El tabaco ornamental florece desde finales de primavera hasta finales de otoño sin necesidad de un mantenimiento particular. Lo importante es elegir bien su variedad. En efecto, una variedad demasiado alta tendría tendencia a colgar, sobre todo si se la expone al viento, y acabaría por perjudicar a las plantas vecinas.

Las calceolarias son conocidas porque pueden causar algunos problemas: en caso de excesiva humedad o de pH demasiado elevado, acusan rápidamente la carencia de hierro. Para evitar el amarilleo de las hojas cloróticas suele bastar un aporte de hierro dirigido. Las calceolarias también son sensibles a la sal, y sus hojas pueden presentar quemaduras fácilmente. Entonces la floración pierde vigor visiblemente.

Las cufeas no florecen generalmente hasta finales de primavera, pero su floración dura hasta las primeras heladas. Resisten muy bien la intemperie y no exigen una limpieza excesiva. Su única debilidad es la de ser muy apreciadas por los pulgones. Un buen pro-

Las hojas de color verde oscuro de las capuchinas contrastan armónicamente con el rojo sangre de sus flores, lo cual es señal de muy buen abono.

ducto fitosanitario remediará fácilmente este problema.

En cuanto a la capuchina, lo más difícil es abonarla bien. Si le aportas una dosis generosa de abono, obtendrás plantas compactas y fuertes, pero su floración dejará que desear. Las plantas que no están bastante nutridas producen gran cantidad de flores, pero sus hojas no son bonitas. Por tanto, es necesario encontrar el justo punto medio. Por último, las onagras florecen sin cesar y sin necesidad de mucho mantenimiento.

Una elegante maceta blanquiazul

Esta nueva composición es el resultado del arreglo de flores de formas y colores de belleza dispar. Los tallos erguidos de la salvia le confieren cierta elegancia. Las panículas de flores azules y blancas plateadas oscilan con ligereza cuando sopla un poco de aire. El contraste de azul y blanco se repite en todo el conjunto, dando a la vez una impresión de calma y de noble discreción. Además, los tonos azules te transmitirán un agradable frescor, incluso en las jornadas más cálidas del verano.

Asociación armónica de plantas

Hemos logrado combinar aquí plantas muy antiguas con nuevas creaciones o con especies recientemente redescubiertas. El resultado es un conjunto natural, armónico y ligero, que no dejará de convertir a tu balcón en el agradable lugar de descanso que sueñas.

Lo que necesitas aquí

① **Dimorfoteca (*Osteospermum ecklonis*), «Polarstern»,** blanca con corazón azul: × 2

② **Salvia azul (*Salvia farinacea*), «Viktoria», azul: × 2**

Cómo plantar

Desde la primera mirada, te encantarán las elegantes panículas de la salvia azul. Esta magnífica planta de balcón desarrolla sus flores azuladas o blancas plateadas sin fatigarse, desde finales de primavera a finales de otoño. Resiste muy bien la intemperie: ni el viento ni la tormenta la afectan.

Plano de la composición de página 19, maceta de 120 × 20 cm

Entre los pies de la salvia se plantan dos dimorfotecas. Esta especie posee flores soberbias cuyo corazón azul reposa como una piedra preciosa en medio de largos pétalos inmaculados. Además, no cesa de florecer a lo largo de todo el verano, aunque en alguna ocasión se tome una pequeña pausa.

En medio de la primera fila, instala la Muraje. Brotará al principio hacia arriba, antes de caer. Esta planta es poco conocida, ya que a finales de primavera, cuando comienza la temporada de los balcones, todavía no tiene flor y pasa desapercibida. Sin embargo, la situación cambia en el curso del verano, durante el cual desarrolla una increíble cantidad de flores de un azul regio espléndido.

La canastillo es la planta de relleno ideal. La variedad «Snowdrift» florece sin cesar en bellos ramos de flores blancas de excelente efecto. Como es una planta cubresuelo, la hemos colocado en el borde de la maceta, desde donde podrá caer formando una bonita mata.

A su lado, las petunias surfinias crecen y florecen de manera desenfrenada hasta constituir verdaderos tapices de flores.

Cómo cuidar tus plantas

La salvia azul, por suerte, no necesita cuidados particulares. Sus panículas perfumadas, sin embargo, tienen tendencia a atraer a los pulgones. Si no hay ningún predador natural para contrarrestarlos, se deberá utilizar un producto preventivo.

Las dimorfotecas experimentan a veces algunas dificultades para florecer, ya que necesitan temperaturas frescas o largas jornadas estivales. Al comprarla, fíjate en que la planta ya tenga numerosos botones bien desarrollados, pues si no fuera así se correría el riesgo de que la floración fuese tardía. El color azul atrae a los trips. Por tanto, no es sorprendente que las flores del muraje ejerzan una atracción casi mágica sobre estos nocivos insectos. Si no son demasiado numerosos, es mejor tolerarlos. En la naturaleza están por todas partes y, de todas maneras, no es posible eliminarlos completamente.

La *Lobularia maritima* (canastillo) tiene una resistencia y una robustez asombrosas. La variedad «Snowdrift» produce además una floración impresionante. En caso de sequía prolongada, o de falta de luz, puede suceder que sus flores caigan. Entonces hará falta un poco de paciencia antes de que florezca de nuevo.

Las panículas azuladas y plateadas de la salvia azul armonizan perfectamente con las begonias de flores rosadas y la verbena.

Las petunias que se obtienen por esqueje resisten de manera sorprendente a la lluvia y a la intemperie. Sin embargo, siempre es preferible protegerlas colocándolas bajo un saliente del techo. Esta planta es conocida por ser ávida y sedienta, lo cual significa que tendrás que abonarla bien y regarla abundantemente. Es aconsejable proporcionarle regularmente un abono completo acidificante. Entonces casi podrás tener la seguridad de que no le faltará hierro.

Dulzura total

He aquí una combinación encantadora de plantas estivales, que prosperarán perfectamente en la fachada oriental de una casa. Nadie puede ser insensible al dulce encanto de sus colores suaves. El rosa y el blanco se fusionan armónicamente, enmarcados por bellos tonos azules. La *Mikania scandens* constituye una especie de nexo, tanto en el plano vertical como en el horizontal. Esta planta de hojas ornamentales contrasta, además, de manera interesante, con sus vecinas. La *Scaevola saligna* no dudará en adherirse a sí misma, y después desarrollará sus flores azules en otras direcciones. Estas dos plantas cortejan activamente a los botones rosados de la diascia, la cual comenzará a brotar hacia arriba antes de volver a caer sobre la parte delantera de la maceta. Durante todo el verano, esta composición no cesará de desarrollar flores. Será la admiración de todos los amantes de las flores.

Lo que necesitas aquí

(1) **Tabaco ornamental** *(Nicotiana × sanderae)*, «Dynamo Weis», blanca: × 3

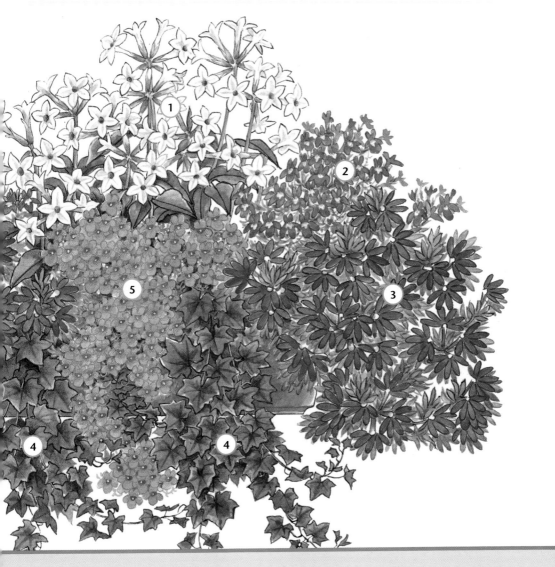

2 Lobelia *(Lobelia valida)*, azul con corazón blanco: × 2

3 *Scaevola saligna*, «New Wonder», azul: × 2

4 *Mikania scandens*, verde: × 2

5 Diascia *(Diascia vigilis)* «Elliott's Variety», rosada: × 1

Cómo plantar

La planta dominante de la fila posterior es, sin duda alguna, el tabaco ornamental blanco. Hemos tratado de escoger una variedad bastante baja y muy robusta: la «Dynamo Weis» crece durante todo el verano hasta alcanzar los 50 cm de altura. Será la compañera ideal de la *Lobelia valida* de flores azules y blancas.

Plano de la composición de página 23, maceta de 100 × 20 cm

Esta última planta, todavía raramente utilizada en balconera, presenta un porte vertical típico, sin alcanzar completamente el tamaño del tabaco ornamental. Sin embargo, sus originales flores, que salen de finales de primavera a principios de otoño, son dignas de admiración.

Directamente delante del tabaco, se colocan las flores rosadas de la diascia. La variedad «Elliott's Variety» comenzará desarrollándose hacia arriba, dirigiendo sus racimos de flores en vertical, antes de dejarlas caer por delante de la maceta. Aunque esta planta sea de apariencia delicada, casi frágil, resiste muy bien a la intemperie. Incluso durante largos periodos de lluvia, su vitalidad natural apenas disminuye. Su floración exuberante no cesa de mediados de primavera a mediados de otoño, y cada flor tiene una increíble duración.

La *Mikania scandens* superará muy pronto el borde de la maceta para descender en cascada. Sus hojas brillantes, verde oscuro, constituyen un fondo perfecto de frescor para las flores rosadas de las Diascia o los tiernos botones azules de la *Scaevola saligna*.

Todos los que ya han cultivado esta última planta, en balconera o en suspensión, no pueden prescindir de ella. Resistente al viento y a la intemperie, mantiene tranquilamente el encanto de sus flores azuladas. Los brotes jóvenes crecen horizontalmente para saltar mejor por encima del borde de la maceta. Las flores nuevas nacen en la axila de las hojas. Si tienes éxito y brota bien, esta planta te ofrecerá una verdadera cascada azul hasta las primeras heladas.

Cómo cuidar tus plantas

La *Mikania scandens* es la planta verde ornamental que marcará el emplazamiento de la maceta, ya que no le gusta la insolación directa, y tiene absoluta necesidad de un poco de sombra durante las horas más cálidas. Si no se tiene esto en cuenta, sus hojas corren el riesgo de que las queme el sol, en particular si no la riegas regularmente. Los tallos y las hojas que se hayan secado deben podarse para evitar botritis o podredumbre. Esta planta soporta fácilmente vivir en sombra.

Éste no es el caso del tabaco ornamental, aunque le gusta estar un poco protegido del sol en medio de la jornada. Sin embargo, las variedades de tabaco de hojas grandes tienen tendencia a marchitarse en caso de una exposición al sol demasiado fuerte, ya que, por lo general, los capilares de las raíces no están en disposición de enviar suficiente agua hasta las hojas. Por otra parte, el tabaco ornamental florece todo el verano sin exigir un gran mantenimiento. Una poda ligera de los tallos después de la primera floración favorecerá la reanudación de la floración. Esto también es válido para la diascia, con la cual suele ser suficiente cortar las inflorescencias marchitas.

Lobelia, diascia y *Scaevola saligna* son todas ellas muy sensibles a la humedad y pre-

El geranio de hiedra y la *Scaevola saligna* no sólo ofrecen una floración ininterrumpida, sino también permiten crear interesantes degradados de colores.

fieren el mantillo ligeramente ácido. Si tu agua de riego es dura y muy calcárea, y si no abonas suficientemente, el pH de tu mantillo corre el riesgo de ser demasiado elevado. Esto implicaría una falta de hierro, visible por el típico amarilleo de las hojas. Por consiguiente, es recomendable utilizar regularmente un abono completo acidificante o un abono especial rico en hierro. De esta forma, se previene o se evita la clorosis.

Contraste de azul y amarillo: luminosidad

Tal como se suele decir, los contrarios se atraen. Por tanto, es necesario comprender el efecto que los colores complementarios ejercen entre ellos, así como la competencia por predominar.

Las plantas participan frecuentemente en este juego de manera natural: no hay más que observar cómo destacan las flores rojas sobre unas hojas de color verde oscuro, y ver cómo se refuerza la luminosidad del rojo. Pero no sólo existe el contraste entre rojo y verde, sino también son parejas conocidas el azul y el naranja, y el amarillo y el violeta.

Una composición al servicio del color

En esta propuesta de maceta, el heliotropo del Perú, de color violeta azulado, enmarca a las margaritas arbustivas amarillas. Es difícil encontrar un contraste más bello. Además se ve reforzado por un conjunto de plantas bajas, todas ellas de colores amarillo y azul. Las especies que hemos escogido prefieren los emplazamientos soleados o, como máximo, a media sombra.

Lo que necesitas aquí

1. Heliotropo *(Heliotropium arborescens)*, *«Marine»*, azul: × 2

2. Margaritas arbustivas *(Argyranthemum frutescens)*, *«Butterfly»*, amarillo: × 2

3 Sanvitalia *(Sanvitalia procumbens)*, «Aztekengold», flores amarillas con corazón marrón: × 2

4 Braquiscome *(Brachyscome multifida)*, «Ultra», azul: × 2

5 Timofilas *(Thymophylla tenuiloba)*, «Sternschnuppe», amarilla: × 1

Cómo plantar

Proponemos utilizar aquí cinco especies diferentes de plantas que se completan unas con otras. En medio, detrás, se plantan dos matas de margarita arbustiva. La variedad «Butterfly» es de un amarillo radiante que destaca desde lejos. Esta planta compacta que se ramifica en abundancia puede crecer hasta 50 cm de altura en el curso del verano, y aumentar otro tanto en anchura.

Plano de la composición de página 27,
maceta de 100 × 20 cm

A derecha e izquierda de las margarita arbustiva, para incrementar aún más su resplandor, se instalan los heliotropos. El heliotropo brota hacia arriba, según la variedad, de 30 a 50 cm. «Marine» forma umbelas de un violeta azulado profundo y despide un intenso perfume de vainilla. Por tanto, no hay que sorprenderse de que las abejas y las mariposas lo aprecien.

Las braquiscomes y las timofilas son dos especies diferentes, pero sólo se distinguen por el color. De formas parecidas, también tienen necesidades idénticas. Crecen hasta unos 20 cm de altura, y forman bonitas cascadas de flores azules y amarillas mezcladas, con una floración incesante.

Por último, en los dos extremos de la maceta hemos plantado la sanvitalia, de flores amarillas delicadas, con corazón marrón, que parecen pequeños girasoles. Como es una planta de tipo cubresuelo, está perfectamente adaptada para escoltar a las margaritas. Entre multitud de variedades que compiten en belleza, la «Aztekengold» ha destacado recientemente.

CONSEJO

Los heliotropos pueden cultivarse fácilmente en maceta e incluso con forma de arbolito. Entonces vale la pena hacerlos invernar. Guárdalos frescos y relativamente secos.

Cómo cuidar tus plantas

Las margaritas arbustivas son plantas muy golosas que exigen un abono rico para que resplandezca su belleza. Si se retiran las flores marchitas, se favorece la formación ininterrumpida de botones. Lamentablemente, las margaritas arbustivas son muy apreciadas por las orugas minadoras, parásitos que atacan sus hojas (galerías, tostadura). Cuando percibas estos síntomas, retira las hojas afectadas, y trata a tus plantas con un producto adecuado. Es difícil de creer, pero el heliotropo y la datilera tienen algo en común: a ambos les gusta tener la copa caliente y las raíces en agua. Por tanto, será necesario ofrecer a los heliotropos un emplazamiento soleado y un mantillo con humedad constante. Si a esta planta perfumada le falta agua durante demasiado tiempo, se le marchitan las hojas. Algunas se secan por completo y adquieren un tinte oscuro. Cuando las umbelas del heliotropo adquieren un color pardo, generalmente es señal de que la primera floración llega a su fin. Córtalas una por una con un par de tijeras para que el conjunto sea agradable a la vista.

Las braquiscomes y las timófilas, al igual que la sanvitalia, prefieren los emplazamientos soleados. A la sombra, las flores son más bien discretas. Estas plantas soportan muy

Flores de formas diferentes: Rudbequia y flox refulgentes de blancura.

mal la humedad o la sequedad excesiva. Si su tierra es demasiado húmeda, sus raíces tienen tendencia a enfermar y sus hojas amarillean. Si olvidas regarlas, puedes tener la seguridad de que una parte de tus plantas morirá. Entonces deberás esperar con paciencia que se regeneren.

Rosa y blanco para un ambiente romántico

Aquí descubrimos una imagen dulce y discreta del verano. El rosa y el blanco se funden mutuamente para formar un ambiente romántico, mientras la variedad de formas de las flores y de las hojas consigue romper cualquier atisbo de monotonía.

Asociación de múltiples especies

Aunque en esta maceta coinciden numerosas especies de plantas, en modo alguno compiten seriamente. En efecto, cada una de ellas utiliza lo mejor posible el espacio de que dispone. La verbena, y también la hiedra terrestre, dejan caer sus tallos con total sencillez por encima del borde de la maceta. En cuanto a la encantadora bacopa, se adapta a todas las situaciones.

Las especies que crecen en vertical mantienen entre sí el apoyo necesario, y excepcionalmente acogen a una flor vecina con sed de libertad. Esta composición prospera mejor al sol o a media sombra.

Lo que necesitas aquí

(1) Dimorfoteca *(Osteospermum ecklonis),* «Henry's Pink», rosada: × 2

(2) Diascia *(Diascia vigilis),* «Elliott's Variety», rosada: × 2

Cómo plantar

En el centro de la fila posterior crecerán las flores dobles de las margaritas arbustivas rosadas. Sin duda, este lugar los valorizará. La variedad «Summer Melody» se ramifica de buen grado, pero sabe permanecer compacta y no sube más de 50 cm, lo cual hace que se adapte particularmente bien a las balconeras.

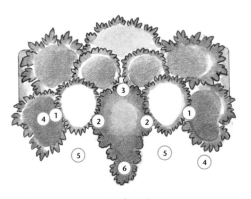

Plano de la composición de página 31, maceta de 100 × 20 cm

Justo delante de las margaritas arbustivas, plantarás dos matas de diascia. Las flores originales de esta escrofulariácea salen sobre largos y elegantes panículos. Dado que brota verticalmente, sus vecinas directas, las margaritas arbustivas y las dimorfo-

tecas, le aportan el sostén necesario para que no se doblen. Podrás comprobar con agradable sorpresa la abundancia de la floración de esta planta, así como su extraordinaria resistencia. El viento y la lluvia apenas afectan a su belleza natural.

Las flores de la dimorfoteca te encantarán realmente. Sus magníficos pétalos de color rosado oscuro se abren bajo los primeros rayos del sol. Lamentablemente, muchas variedades necesitan una gran pausa entre dos floraciones. Sin embargo, las nuevas variedades prometen una mejoría al respecto.

La hiedra terrestre es una planta verde ornamental de las más interesantes. Sus finos tallos brotan casi en vertical hacia abajo, produciendo una elegante cascada verde, que puede alcanzar hasta dos metros en el curso del verano.

Las flores de las nuevas variedades de *Sutera* son más grandes y mucho más numerosas. Como esta planta es originalmente un cubresuelo, forma magníficas matas, siempre muy apreciadas en los balcones.

Por último, la verbena, de flores color rosado viejo, no dudará en sobrepasar el borde de la maceta para redondear suavemente los ángulos de nuestra composición perfumada. Además, esta planta exquisita es muy apreciada por las mariposas.

Cómo cuidar tus plantas

Las margaritas arbustivas de flores rosadas deben limpiarse de vez en cuando. Las flores marchitas tienen tendencia a oscurecerse, y acabarían por estropear el conjunto de la composición. Aprecian el sol y también necesitan sustancias nutritivas permanentemente. A su lado las aparentemente débiles diascias son realmente de una resistencia y de una robustez sorprendentes. Sin embargo, soportan mal los excesos de humedad. Un riego demasiado abundante, o una evacuación defectuosa, pueden provocar fácilmente el ennegrecimiento y la muerte de los tallos. Es recomendable cortar los racimos de flores marchitas o secas para favorecer una nueva floración.

Las dimorfotecas resisten al viento y a la lluvia. Estas plantas no necesitan un mantenimiento particular, aparte de la limpieza de las flores marchitas. Al comprarlas, fíjate en que tus plantas presenten numerosos botones, si no quieres que se retrase la floración. A las dimorfotecas les gusta brillar bajo el sol antes de abrir perfectamente sus flores. Los rayos matinales no dejarán de motivarlas.

Afortunadamente las nuevas variedades de verbena resisten muy bien al oidio.

Armónica superposición de un tono sobre otro, de belleza suave y discreta pero bien visible.

Sin embargo, puede suceder que, con las primeras noches frescas, o incluso durante un largo periodo de mal tiempo, las hojas se cubran con el típico polvo blancuzco. Al regar, hay que procurar que las hojas tengan tiempo de secarse en el curso de la jornada y que no estén húmedas al llegar la noche. Además, están las delicadas bacopas cuya capacidad de adaptación te sorprenderá. Tan sólo la sombra puede hacer peligrar su floración. Evita que se seque su mantillo.

En cuanto a la hiedra terrestre, es una planta extremadamente robusta que no necesita mantenimiento particular.

Rojo y blanco, poderosa oposición

En esta nueva composición, la tradición convive con la novedad. Las flores son de color rojo o blanco. En el curso del verano, su luminosa belleza será visible desde lejos. Todas las especies utilizadas prefieren crecer al sol o, como mucho, a media sombra. Los geranios zonales representan con fuerza el papel principal. Una vez más, se muestran capaces de sostener el conjunto de una composición, permitiendo, por ejemplo, que los claveles ofrezcan una pausa entre dos floraciones.

Especies clásicas, pero asociaciones nuevas

Las nuevas variedades de verbena ofrecen una floración tan abundante que no es posible dejar de apreciarlas. Las hojas de reflejos plateados de la inmortal cautivan la mirada, sin que ello impida que la bacopa se desarrolle con todo su esplendor.

Lo que necesitas aquí

1. **Geranio zonal** *(Pelargonium × hortorum)*, Tango «Dark Red», rojo: × 3

2. **Clavel de China** *(Dianthus × chinensis)*, «Telstar White», blanco: × 2

3. **Verbena** *(Verbena, híbrido)*, Tukana «Scarlet», roja: × 2

4. **Bacopa** *(Sutera grandiflora)*, «Blizzard», blanca: × 2

5. **Siempreviva** *(Helichrysum petiolare)*, «Mini Silver», follaje tipo fieltro, blanca plateada: × 1

Cómo plantar

Las plantas que hemos utilizado son conocidas desde hace mucho tiempo, pero se presentan en esta maceta bajo un nuevo aspecto. La última serie de geranios, en su variedad Tango, impresiona desde la primera mirada. Sus flores rojo bermellón contrastan en belleza con el verde oscuro de su follaje. Al ser esta planta muy compacta, deberás vigilar para que las especies vecinas no crezcan demasiado y entren en competencia con ella.

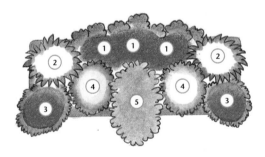

Plano de la composición de página 35, maceta de 100 × 20 cm

Los claveles de China serán, bajo esta óptica, vecinos leales y no sobrepasarán en tamaño el límite que les hayamos im-puesto. Sus delicadas flores blancas no sólo son encantadoras, sino también su-brayan con su presencia la belleza de los geranios.

La primera fila repite la misma oposición entre rojo y blanco, pero esta vez según una disposición inversa. Así instalarás las flores escarlatas de la verbena en los extremos de la maceta, allá donde podrán desplegarse alegremente. La nueva variedad Tukana «Scarlet», de un rojo vivo magnífico, no dejará de complacerte, ya que florece muy pronto. Desarrolla rápidamente una verdadera cascada florida y no cesa de crecer a lo largo de todo el verano.

Después hemos plantado nuestra bacopa en medio, para estar seguros de que la verbena y los geranios no se disimularán unos con otros, y jugarán plenamente el papel que se les ha asignado. La *Sutera grandiflora* valoriza a sus vecinas como ninguna otra planta pueda hacerlo. En esto le ayuda la siempreviva, en el centro de la primera fila. Esta planta, discreta, aporta un toque de elegancia a la composición. La variedad «Mini Silver» parece particularmente adaptada a nuestra maceta. En efecto, las otras variedades son mucho más imponentes y tienen cierta tendencia a ser invasoras.

Cómo cuidar tus plantas

Comienza por escoger un buen emplazamiento, ya que esta composición no se desarrollará con todo su esplendor más que al sol o, como máximo, a media sombra, si a pesar de todo el lugar está bien iluminado. Una vez establecido este punto, el conjunto de especies utilizadas es fácil de mantener y no presenta problemas especiales. Con excepción de la bacopa, todas las plantas son bastante ávidas, y necesitan que se les aporte regularmente sustancias nutritivas. Si no las abonas suficientemente, tendrán dificultades para producir una floración normal. Es aconsejable retirar las umbelas marchitas de los geranios, no sólo por razones estéticas, sino también para evitar que se pudran las flores.

Los claveles de China, al igual que los geranios, soportan mal los excesos de humedad. Así pues, no olvides dosificar bien el riego. Por lo general, a principios de verano es la época en que la floración de los claveles es más bella. Cuando aparezcan las primeras flores marchitas, es recomendable comenzar a limpiarlas, con el fin de favorecer la reanudación floral.

La verbena, por su parte, no hace pausa alguna, a menos que uno se olvide de abonarla o de regarla durante demasiado tiempo. Además, las nuevas variedades han sido mejora-

La presencia de la siempreviva confiere a esta maceta de petunias una belleza muy particular.

das, y no sufren del oidio tanto como las antiguas. Sin embargo, procura que las hojas de tu planta tengan tiempo para secarse en el curso de la jornada, y no estén húmedas al llegar la noche, lo cual favorecería las enfermedades criptogámicas.

Aunque la sutera casi no necesite cuidado alguno, requiere un mínimo de atención. Un exceso de humedad implicará el amarilleo de sus hojas (clorosis), y en casos extremos, enfermedades a nivel de las raíces, pudiendo llegar incluso a la muerte de la planta. Por el contrario, si no la riegas suficientemente, la floración dejará que desear, y ciertas partes de la planta se secarán.

Para concluir, la siempreviva es una planta muy robusta y poco exigente que no necesita mantenimiento alguno.

Los colores de la alegría de vivir

Si buscas nuevas combinaciones de colores, aconsejaríamos que siguieses la teoría del color. De esta manera, tendrías la seguridad de no equivocarte. Es así de sencillo, los colores que armonizan unos con otros se encuentran en los vértices del triángulo equilátero inscrito dentro del círculo cromático. Es una combinación de tres tonalidades. Si eliges bien tus colores, podrás obtener los efectos más diversos: tonos intensos y suaves, fríos y cálidos. Cada matiz actúa de manera diferente sobre el espectador.

Color y gusto

Nuestra composición de color amarillo, rojo y azul respira la alegría de vivir, sin ser demasiado estridente. El color blanco sirve sobre todo para establecer el nexo entre los dos tonos diferentes de azul. Todas las especies utilizadas aprecian los emplazamientos soleados o, al menos, a media sombra.

Lo que necesitas aquí

1. Geranio zonal *(Pelargonium × hortorum)*, «Avenida», rojo luminoso: × 2
2. Salvia azul *(Salvia farinacea)*, «Viktoria», azul: × 2

(3) Tagetes *(Tagetes tenuifolia)*, «Lulu», amarillo: × 1

(4) Campanilla azul *(Convolvulus sabatius)*, «Blaue Mauritius», azul claro: × 1

(5) Torenia *(Torenia fournieri)*, Summer wave, «Large Blue», azul: × 2

(6) Agerato *(Ageratum houstonianum)*, «White Hawai», blanco: × 2

Cómo plantar

En esta maceta hemos asociado seis especies diferentes de plantas. En el centro de la fila posterior, hemos colocado los tagetes, los cuales formarán en el curso del verano una mata casi esférica constituida por innumerables florecitas amarillas. Su fino follaje entrelazado y su porte libre dan la impresión de que se trata de una flor silvestre.

Plano de la composición de página 39, maceta de 100 × 20 cm

La salvia azul tiene una apariencia completamente diferente. Sus finos panículos azules se estiran hacia el cielo, separando el amarillo de los claveles y el rojo luminoso de los geranios «Avenida». Hemos colocado a estos últimos en los extremos de la fila. Ro-

bustos, crecerán rápidamente y florecerán sin fallo hasta otoño, dos preciosas cualidades.

La campanilla azul desprende un soplo de exotismo. Lamentablemente, sus flores sólo se abren bajo los rayos del sol. Cuando el cielo está demasiado cubierto, o en tiempo de lluvia, no podrás apreciar su belleza, pero quizás en esto consista el encanto de esta planta y lo que la hace tan interesante. Al comprarla, fíjate en que presente abundantes botones, pues en caso contrario se correría el riesgo de retraso en la floración.

Luego la mirada se posará sobre la blancura del agerato, que constituye un puente entre las diferentes manchas de color. Planta tupida, compacta, con una floración muy abundante, rellena los espacios vacíos de manera ideal en una maceta muy coloreada por otra parte. Aquí sirve de agradable nexo entre los diferentes tonos de azul de la enredadera y de los híbridos de torenia.

C O N S E J O

Las torenias padecen frecuentemente clorosis, caracterizada por un amarilleo de las hojas jóvenes, mientras sus vetas todavía permanecen verdes. Para evitar este problema, añade un abono especial, rico en hierro, a tu agua de riego.

Cómo cuidar tus plantas

Los diminutos tagetes, cuyas flores son pequeñas y simples, exigen menos cuidados que las variedades de flores dobles, por ejemplo. No obstante, hay que entender bien que, siguiendo las normas de la buena jardinería, eso no dispensa de regarlos y abonarlos regularmente. La salvia azul tiene la misma necesidad. Por su parte, algunas veces sus panículos son colonizados por los pulgones. Para combatirlos, puede ser suficiente cortar los tallos afectados, y utilizar un insecticida biológico apropiado. Normalmente, el tallo principal de las matas de salvia azul se corta para favorecer el brote de los tallos laterales. Si no se ha hecho esto, no dudes en poner remedio personalmente.

Los geranios prefieren los emplazamientos soleados y, si es posible, a resguardo de la lluvia. Son plantas bastante ávidas de abono, que soportan bien la sequía. Para evitar la podredumbre de las flores, quítales las umbelas cuando estén marchitas.

La campanilla azul necesita mucho sol, pues si no es así, no se abrirán completamente sus encantadoras flores. Por tanto, es muy importante que escojas bien su emplazamiento. Por otra parte, esta planta requiere muy pocos cuidados.

Los ageratos, por el contrario, deben lim-

Las torenias prefieren los emplazamientos cálidos y protegidos. En suspensión, estas plantas producen una enorme cantidad de flores.

piarse de vez en cuando. Las variedades de flores blancas, en particular, tienen tendencia a ennegrecerse cuando se marchitan. Pero no hay que quitarlas sólo por razones estéticas, sino, sobre todo, para que las nuevas flores tengan espacio para desarrollarse.

Las torenias, por último, prefieren los veranos cálidos, pasados a resguardo del viento y de la lluvia. Si las abonas correctamente y las riegas en abundancia, formarán magníficas matas de flores.

Plantas de sombra

La mayoría de plantas de jardín o de balcón prefieren los emplazamientos soleados o a media sombra. Pero si tu balcón está constantemente a la sombra, no es una razón para renunciar al placer de tener flores en tu casa. Es cierto que tendrás que escoger entre un número reducido de especies, pero serán suficientes para alegrar el ambiente.

Plantas clásicas de sombra

Las plantas de balcón que son bien conocidas para soportar la sombra son las begonias, las fucsias, las alegrías de Nueva Guinea, y también numerosas plantas verdes ornamentales. Además, no hay que olvidar que ciertas especies de adaptación fácil son muy capaces de tolerar una vida a la sombra.

En esta composición, hemos ensayado asociar colores claros y alegres, capaces de iluminar tu balcón: tonos amarillos, albaricoque, carmín, cuyos matices son visibles de lejos y caldean la atmósfera, con tanto acierto que incluso un balcón orientado al norte se transformará en un vigorizante oasis.

Lo que necesitas aquí

1 **Begonia tuberosa de porte erguido (grupo** *Begonia tuberhybrida***),** «Nonstop Goldorange», naranja luminosa: × 4

2 Begonia colgante (grupo *Begonia tuberhybrida*), «Illumination Apricot», color albaricoque: × 2

6 Alegrías de Nueva Guínea (Alegrías × «Nueva Guínea), Paraíso «Martinique», rojo carmín: × 2

8 Fucsia (*Fuchsia*, híbrido), «Presidente Georg Bartlett», magenta/violeta: × 1

Cómo plantar

La composición que proponemos comprende nueve plantas en total. La combinación de los colores escogidos da una impresión de calor y de luminosidad, debida en particular a la presencia de las begonias de porte erguido. En efecto, hemos plantado cuatro matas de color naranja vivo que llenan la segunda fila.

Plano de la composición de página 43, maceta de 100 × 20 cm

Tal como indica el nombre de su variedad (Begonia «Nonstop»), florecen sin cesar desde finales de primavera hasta las primeras heladas. Unos tallos sólidos y cortos soportan sus espléndidas flores dobles, lo cual garantiza gran resistencia a la intemperie. Al efectuar la plantación, se ha de procurar instalar las plantas ni demasiado altas ni demasiado profundas.

Los tubérculos deben estar cubiertos por una fina capa de tierra. Si las plantas demasiado cerca de la superficie, tu planta corre el riesgo de no sostenerse bien de pie, y te será difícil regarla. Y si la plantas demasiado profunda, el cuello de la raíz corre mucho más riesgo de caer enfermo. Esto también es válido para las begonias colgantes que plantarás en primera fila. Estas begonias son muy imponentes y bastante espectaculares. La variedad que hemos utilizado desarrolla bellas flores de color albaricoque teñidas de amarillo, de 10 cm de ancho. El porte de la variedad «Illumination Apricot» es relativamente compacto en comparación con sus vecinas, pero sus flores luminosas sobrepasan a todas las otras. Justo al lado, hemos instalado otras dos plantas de sombra bien conocidas: las alegrías de Nueva Guínea con sus bonitas flores rojo carmín y la fucsia colgante con sus delicadas flores de cáliz magenta y de corola violeta. Estas dos especies de plantas ofrecen posibilidades muy numerosas: hay más de 2.000 variedades de fucsias, y los tipos de alegrías son casi tan numerosos.

Cómo cuidar tus plantas

Pocas plantas hay que reclamen tan poco mantenimiento y produzcan una floración tan abundante como las begonias de porte erguido. Sus flores resisten de manera sorprendente la lluvia, pero pesan tanto que algunas veces amenazan la estabilidad de la planta. Los tallos carnosos de las begonias son muy frágiles. También es recomendable no exponerlas al viento. Esta especie aprecia un mantillo de humedad constante, no dudes pues en utilizar una maceta con depósito de agua. Las raicillas buscan agua sin cesar, así como sustancias nutritivas para favorecer el crecimiento.

Las alegrías de Nueva Guinea prefieren los emplazamientos cálidos y protegidos. Florecen tan bien a la sombra como a media sombra. Sin embargo, algunas variedades aceptan vivir al sol si se las riega suficientemente. Por lo general las alegrías siempre tienen sed, y les es muy difícil renunciar a su riego cotidiano. El menor periodo de sequía hace que se marchiten. Si esto sucede, apresúrate a suministrar agua, a fin de evitar lo peor. Por último, en caso de un periodo largo de mal tiempo, es aconsejable cortar las flores marchitas para evitar su podredumbre.

Las fucsias son plantas tradicionales de balcón. Para evitar que hagan pausas demasiado largas entre dos floraciones, aconsejamos regarlas y abonarlas bien. Las plantas débiles o subalimentadas son víctimas frecuentemente de botritis o de roya. Limpia tus fucsias de vez en cuando. Al hacerlo, retira las flores marchitas para evitar que la planta se agote al producir las semillas. Aprovecha entonces para verificar que no haya sido atacada por algún insecto nocivo: en efecto, las fucsias son apreciadas por las moscas blancas, los pulgones y las arañas rojas.

Los colores vivos y cálidos de las begonias colgantes iluminarán tus macetas colocadas a la sombra.

Una balconera perfumada

El perfume del Mediterráneo nos evoca frecuentemente recuerdos agradables. Así pues, ¿por qué no llevar el sur a nuestro balcón? ¿Por qué no podemos cerrar los ojos y dejarnos invadir por la magia de los olores? Por consiguiente, respira los aromas de los matorrales, la lavanda, la vainilla, perfume de vacaciones, de calma y de descanso. Abre, incluso, tus ventanas y tus puertas para que estos deliciosos olores penetren en tu casa.

Perfumes del atardecer

Son numerosas las plantas que sólo propagan su perfume por la tarde o después de una lluvia cálida. Entonces, ¿cómo resistir a la llamada del balcón? Disfrutarás de las más bellas horas del día con un espíritu de plena relajación. Aprovecha también el maravilloso espectáculo que te ofrece cada planta viéndola crecer: renovando sus flores sin cesar, con el encaje de sus hojas, con las abejas y las mariposas que se acercan para visitarlas.

Lo que necesitas aquí

1. **Siempreviva amarilla (Helichrysum italicum),** flores amarillas, hojas gris plateado: × 2

2. **Heliotropo (Heliotropium arborescens),** «Marine», azul: × 3

3. Tomillo limón *(Thymus × citriodorus)*, hojas verdes y blancas: × 2

4. Lavanda *(Lavandula angustifolia)*, «Hidcote Blue»: × 2

5. Plectranto *(Plectranthus forsteri)*, hojas blancas y verdes: × 1

Cómo plantar

Esta espléndida composición reúne cinco especies de aromas diferentes, que expanden un perfume ricamente especiado, que sólo se puede percibir en la región mediterránea. Además, el predominio de los tonos azules crea un ambiente de calma y descanso.

Del heliotropo emana un suave perfume de vainilla. Según las variedades, esta planta de porte erguido puede alcanzar 50 cm. Hemos decidido que aquí fuera la planta predominante, ya que ha superado sus pruebas de desarrollo desde hace años sin doblar sus umbelas de color azul profundo. La variedad «Marine», más alta, es más adecuada para la fila posterior de la maceta que, por ejemplo, la «Mini-Marine», mucho más compacta.

A derecha e izquierda, plantarás la siempreviva amarilla, cuyo delicado follaje plateado atraerá irremediablemente las miradas. Es cierto que sus pequeñas flores amarillas aparecerán probablemente por la tarde y sin redobles de tambor. Pero basta coger una hoja y frotarla entre el pulgar y el índice para respirar el perfume de los matorrales.

Las hojas del tomillo limón también son refrescantes. Esta planta forma matas, y por ello es adecuada para colocarla en primera

Plano de la composición de página 47, maceta de 100 × 20 cm

fila. Sus flores son muy discretas, pero sus delicadas hojas blancas y verdes son muy elegantes. Las plantas jóvenes de lavanda crecen con relativa lentitud para alcanzar unos 40 cm en otoño. Los panículos de flores azuladas se destacan con elegancia del follaje gris plateado de esta planta aromática, cuyo intenso perfume es bien conocido.

De la plectranto emana un olor de incienso, lo cual le ha valido para ser llamada *planta del incienso* en ciertas regiones. Su perfume no gusta a todo el mundo, pero también es seductora por su porte y por el delicado dibujo de sus hojas.

Cómo cuidar
tus plantas

Todas las plantas de esta balconera aprecian el sol y el calor. Tanto si se trata de la siempreviva, como de la lavanda o del tomillo limón, todas exigen muy pocos cuidados. Ofréceles un buen emplazamiento. Después, bastará regarlas y abonarlas regularmente. Evita a toda costa los excesos de humedad.

La plectranto es una planta de balcón particularmente robusta. En otoño, sus tallos, siempre tan bellos, pueden alcanzar dos metros de largo, mientras numerosas especies ya se han tomado vacaciones.

Sólo el heliotropo es un poco más caprichoso que sus vecinas. Para que se desarrolle bien, debes regarlo con verdadera regularidad. Cuando le falta agua, sus hojas se echan a perder, se desecan literalmente y adquieren un tinte casi negro. Una maceta con reserva de agua será útil al respecto. Por otra parte, las umbelas marchitas del heliotropo se ennegrecen. Por tanto, es recomendable cortarlas para favorecer la reanudación de la floración. Si lo deseas, al final de temporada puedes tras-

Los geranios de olor presentan una floración menos abundante que los otros, pero sus flores son muy bellas. La variedad «Citronella» desprende un suave perfume a limón.

plantar tu heliotropo y conservarlo todo el invierno en un lugar claro y fresco.

Si eres bastante hábil, puedes reutilizar la planta al año siguiente o seguir cultivándola en maceta.

La lavanda, por el contrario, debe permanecer en el exterior al final de la temporada. Si la plantas en tu jardín, esta vivaz vivirá varios años. Soporta muy bien el invierno, aunque no es aconsejable que lo pase en maceta, ya que sus raíces corren el riesgo de helarse y la planta el de secarse.

Otras sugerencias

Puedes reemplazar:

(2) por Geranio de olor *(Pelargonium × hortorum)* «Citronella», pétalos rosados manchados: × 3. Esta planta desprende un suave olor a limón.

Una jardinera especial para los gastrónomos

Cuando se cultivan hierbas y verduras en el balcón, es natural querer recolectarlas.
Si eres principiante, comienza por verduras fáciles de cultivar, mientras adquieres experiencia. Los jardineros experimentados ya saben, por su parte, que prácticamente en maceta puede cultivarse casi todo.

Algunos consejos para la composición

De la misma manera que para la elaboración de una maceta de flores, debes prestar atención aquí al porte de la planta, al color de sus hojas y de sus frutos, tanto como a sus flores. Uitliza todo el espacio de que dispongas en todas direcciones. Escoge plantas dominantes de alto porte vertical para la fila posterior, y plantas más bajas o colgantes para la primera fila. Así tendrás la seguridad de ocupar tu maceta de manera óptima. La regla más importante es la siguiente: coloca una planta cada diez centímetros. Si te apetece, puedes introducir flores de verano coloreadas en tu maceta hortelana. Causará un efecto excelente.

Lo que necesitas aquí

1. Maíz dulce *(Zea mays)*: × 4
2. Pera-melón *(Solanum muricatum)* «Pepino-Gold»: × 1
3. Eneldo *(Anethum graveolens)*: × 1
4. Tomate *(Lycopersicon esculentum)* «Balkonstar»: × 1

5 Acelga *(Beta vulgaris)* «Feurio»: × 1

6 Tomillo *(Thymus vulgaris)*: × 1

7 Albahaca *(Ocimum tenuiflorum)*: × 1

8 Orégano *(Origanum vulgare)*: × 1

9 Romero *(Rosmarinus officinalis)*: × 1

10 Lobelia *(Lobelia erinus)*, por ej. Temptation «Skyblue», azul: × 1

Cómo plantar

No todos los balcones se adaptan al cultivo de verduras y de hierbas aromáticas. Cuanto más claro y soleado sea tu balcón, más bonito será el crecimiento y mayor será tu cosecha. La mejor orientación es al este o al oeste. Los balcones situados a la sombra son menos convenientes. En cuanto a los orientados al sur, pueden llegar a ser muy pronto demasiado cálidos si no se les riega adecuadamente.

Además, muchas verduras prefieren crecer a resguardo del viento. Hay que evitar también los balcones que den a calles con mucho tránsito. Si cultivas tus propias verduras, se debe vigilar que la polución no las contamine, y que sigan sanas.

Por consiguiente, planta en la segunda fila de tu maceta el melón-pera, la acelga, el eneldo, el maíz y los tomates. En la parte delantera de tu minihuerto, instala las hierbas aromáticas: romero, albahaca, orégano y tomillo. Por último, añade una lobelia azul a la composición.

De acuerdo con el arreglo descrito, esta balconera puede competir con la mejor maceta florida. Es imposible dejar de admirar la imponente planta de maíz que crece muy deprisa hasta un metro de altura. Con el eneldo, constituye el punto fuerte del conjunto.

La acelga no es menos interesante. Esta verdura de raíz carnosa presenta hojas muy bonitas. Sola en un tiesto, puede crecer hasta 80 cm de altura, aunque en balconera suele ser más discreta.

Plano de la composición de página 51, maceta de 100 × 20 cm

Cultiva los tomates y los peras-melones en pirámide, sin tutores. Será lo más sencillo. Las frutas colgarán por encima del borde de la maceta, en cada uno de sus extremos, allí donde hayas instalado las plantas. Como tendrás tomates, no puedes dejar de plantar albahaca. Dado que casi todas las plantas se cultivan muy fácilmente en balconera, la elección de tus plantas aromáticas depende de lo que pienses cocinar.

Cómo cuidar tus plantas

El maíz produce de una a dos mazorcas por planta, las cuales están maduras cuando su plumero adquiere un color tostado. Entonces podrás hacerlas a la plancha, hervidas o incluso comerlas crudas. Entre las variedades más dulces figuran la «Golden Supersweet» y la «Early Extra Sweet».

El eneldo se vende principalmente picado en pequeños frascos. Cuando comienza a florecer, es aconsejable ponerle tutores para impedir que se desplome. En cocina, se utilizan las hojas y las flores finamente picadas en salsas, ensaladas, o para perfumar el pescado.

La acelga se prepara como los espárragos o las espinacas. Recoléctala en función de tus necesidades. Así dispondrás siempre de hojas frescas y no marchitas para cocinar.

A los tomates les gusta estar protegidos de la lluvia. Si sus hojas se mojan demasiado frecuentemente pueden pudrirse o ser invadidos por la *Phytophthora infestans*. Ésta es la razón por la cual es necesario regar a pie de planta. La «estrella» de nuestra balconera es una mata de tomate breñoso. Para que no se desgarre bajo el peso de sus frutos y perma-

Estéticamente, esta «maceta hortofrutícola» puede competir con cualquier balconera de flores.

nezca estable puede recurrirse a un tutor de bambú. Recolecta los tomates cuando estén bien rojos y maduros, ya que en ese momento tienen su mejor sabor.

Pon un tutor al pera-melón, pero siguiendo su porte breñoso. En general, el mejor momento para recolectar los frutos es cuando amarillean, hacia finales de verano. Los pera-melón se comen frescos, pero también puedes hacer confitura.

Las plantas aromáticas utilizadas en nuestro ejemplo no requieren ningún cuidado particular. Un riego regular y un abono consecuente son suficientes para obtener buenos resultados. Esto mismo es aplicable, por otra parte, a la lobelia.

Otras sugerencias

Puedes reemplazar:

(2) **por guindilla** *(Capsicum annuum)*
Sus bonitos frutos difieren en función de las variedades: más o menos picantes, pueden ser amarillos, anaranjados o rojos. La variedad «Medusa», por ejemplo, es un pimiento dulce, mientras que «Cheyenne» es mucho más fuerte.

Pequeña guía práctica

Compras

Las plantas de macizo y de balcón se ponen a la venta –y se compran– desde mediados de primavera, mientras que antes se esperaba al deshielo para comenzar la temporada de los balcones. El comportamiento de los jardineros ha cambiado. Cada uno espera el verano con impaciencia, y quiere que su balcón esté a punto para el inicio de la temporada. El entusiasmo prematuro tropieza a veces con heladas tardías, y entonces de han de cubrir las plantas y se llega a tener que introducir las macetas de nuevo en el interior.

Macetas

Es importante que tus plantas dispongan de un volumen suficiente de mantillo, que pueda aportar a sus raíces la cantidad de agua y de sustancias nutritivas correspondientes a sus necesidades. Por tanto, recomendamos balconeras de 20 cm de anchura y de 20 cm de profundidad. Fíjate en que posean un buen sistema de evacuación de agua, ya que no es raro que las plantas se «ahoguen» en el sentido literal de la palabra. Para evitar los excesos de humedad, verifica regularmente que los orificios de evacuación no estén obstruidos. Piensa en colocar tiestos de barro cocido en tu maceta, pues te será útil.

Mantillo

Si compras plantas de alta calidad, no trates de economizar con el mantillo. Un buen mantillo debe contener todas las sustancias nutritivas y los oligoelementos necesarios para tus flores. Por lo general, es capaz de alimentar a tus plantas durante 3 a 4 semanas, de modo que no tengas que abonarlas hasta después de la plantación. La arcilla que contiene se encarga de repartir regularmente el agua en toda la maceta, y permite evitar eventuales quemaduras de las raíces si has abonado en exceso. Los mantillos universales que se venden en jardinería cumplen todas estas condiciones. Se necesitan alrededor de 35 litros de mantillo para una jardinera de flores de un metro de largo por 20 cm de ancho y de alto. Si utilizas compost casero, piensa en analizarlo previamente, pues frecuentemente es demasiado rico en salario o

Si compras plantas de calidad, es importante que inviertas en un mantillo de calidad.

Cómo plantar, paso a paso: retirando los terrones, verifica que las raíces estén blancas y sanas.

Instala los terrones ni demasiado cerca de la superficie ni demasiado profundos.

Después de haber acabado, riega abundantemente.

presenta un pH demasiado elevado.

Además, podría ser que tuviera hongos o enfermedades que harían peligrar tus plantaciones.

La plantación

Antes de plantar, es aconsejable sumergir en agua los terrones de las plantas que se puedan desecar. Luego hay que vigilar a qué profundidad instalas tus plantas: demasiado cerca de la superficie, las raíces corren el riesgo de secarse muy pronto y de que la planta padezca por falta de agua. Demasiado profundamente, el cuello de las raíces corre el riesgo de pudrirse. Hay que prever una reguera de 2 cm para un riego más sencillo. Por último, después de haber compactado la tierra alrededor de la planta, riega abundantemente. Tu balconera está a punto.

Reglas de composición

Una de las reglas más importantes en la creación de una balconera consiste en tener en cuenta el porte de cada planta. En la mayoría de casos, las especies altas y de porte erguido se colocarán detrás. En los espacios vacíos, instalarás las plantas más bajas, y después en primer plano las especies colgantes.

Es necesario dejar suficiente espacio para el riego.

Los especialistas diferencian así las plantas dominantes −con efecto garantizado y que constituyen la estructura básica de la composición− de las plantas de relleno, que valorizan a las anteriores y aportan variedad a los conjuntos. Por otra parte, todas las plantas de macizo cubresuelo pueden utilizarse en maceta como plantas colgantes. Así pues, existen numerosas posibilidades de composición, tanto en altura como en profundidad.

Abono

Un aporte de sustancias nutritivas y un riego suficiente, he aquí la clave de tu éxito. Las plantas consumen rápidamente las sustancias nutritivas presentes en el mantillo. Por tanto, es necesario aportar otras nuevas a las raíces. Debes abonar las macetas, al menos cada diez días, con dos o tres gramos de fertilizante completo por litro de agua. Por lo general, para una maceta de un metro de largo, 10 gramos de fertilizante (Composición: nitrógeno/fósforo/potasa: 15-11-15) disueltos en cinco litros de agua, será suficiente. A lo largo de las doce semanas del verano, se distribuyen alrededor de 50 a 75 gramos de abono por metro de maceta. Si la tarea te parece pesada, o si no tienes tiempo, es mejor recurrir a un abono de liberación lenta que puedas mezclar con tu mantillo desde el principio.

La clave del éxito: abonar regularmente las balconeras.

En este caso, cinco gramos de abono de liberación lenta por litro de mantillo son suficientes para responder a las necesidades de sustancias nutritivas de las plantas durante toda la temporada. Las sustancias nutritivas se liberarán progresivamente en función de la humedad del mantillo y de la temperatura.

Desde hace cierto tiempo, este tipo de abono existe también bajo forma de bastoncitos, y basta plantarlos en el mantillo húmedo. Recientemente también se han empezado a vender bolitas de abono. Sigue siempre las instrucciones que acompañan a los productos.

Riego

En una jornada cálida de verano se necesitan a veces hasta diez litros de agua por metro de balconera. Esto significa que, en una situación extrema, un solo riego no basta para calmar la sed de las plantas. Para que regar no se convierta en una carga, quizá puedas

considerar la compra de un sistema de riego automático o semiautomático. Existen tres tipos.

Macetas con reservas de agua e irrigación por mechas

Un doble fondo en el interior de la maceta separa la reserva de agua del mantillo. El agua se transporta de abajo hacia arriba hasta las raíces por medio de mechas absorbentes. Según las macetas, el depósito puede contener hasta diez litros de agua, lo cual es suficiente para alimentar a una planta durante un fin de semana prolongado, o sencillamente para aligerar la carga del riego.

La maceta se llena por medio de una regadera o de una manguera conectada a un tubo. Un indicador, o una ventanilla, permite controlar el nivel del agua. Es importante que funcione el sistema de evacuación cuando el agua llegue a un nivel excesivo, para no correr el riesgo

Una balconera con reserva de agua sobrevivirá fácilmente a un fin de semana sin riego.

de perjudicar las raíces. Existen también macetas que se pueden conectar en serie por medio de mangueras. Una primera maceta de mando contiene un flotador que hace funcionar automáticamente el llenado de las macetas cuando se ha alcanzado un nivel mínimo.

Los goteros del sistema Blumat reaccionan individualmente según el nivel de humedad del suelo.

Por lo general esta maceta está directamente conectada a una toma de agua. Vigila sobre todo que el conjunto de tus balconeras esté bien horizontal y a la misma altura. Un sistema como éste puede hacerse cargo del riego de tu balcón durante todo el verano.

Goteros autorregulables

Los goteros reaccionan individualmente a la humedad del suelo. Este sistema es particularmente práctico cuando se deben regar varios tiestos con necesidades diferentes. Importa poco que las balconeras se encuentren a la sombra o al sol.

Estos aparatos funcionan con una toma de agua, un reductor de presión que hace de cedazo, y un tubo de distribución dotado de goteros. El nivel de humedad del mantillo se estima directamente a la salida del agua gracias a unos conos de arcilla (sistema Blumat) o de madera. Además, cada gote-ro puede regularse con precisión por medio de un tornillo de ajuste.

Por tanto, el jardinero puede aumentar o reducir el número de gotas de agua que llegan a su maceta.

Riego con válvula eléctrica

Este sistema de riego necesita una toma de agua y una alimentación eléctrica de exteriores. Se conecta al grifo una válvula eléctrica de 24 voltios y un reductor de presión para disminuir la presión del agua a un bar. El riego se activa automáticamente a través de un detector de humedad (tensiómetro) y un programador. Puedes decidir la cantidad de agua fijando la duración del riego y el número de goteros. Si no dispones de toma eléctrica exterior, puedes utilizar un sencillo programador a pilas. Este aparato se fija directamente sobre el grifo, y funciona con un detector de humedad o con un temporizador. Es posible programar hasta seis riegos diarios.

Evidentemente, estos sistemas de riego pueden adaptarse tanto a los arriates de flores como a los huertos o los invernaderos. Pueden servir incluso para regar el césped. Nada hay que temer al respecto, pues no es necesario ser un técnico experimentado para hacerlos funcionar.

Limpieza y poda

Aunque sólo sea por razones estéticas, las inflorescencias marchitas no han de tener lugar alguno en tus balconeras. Las flores dobles, por ejemplo, tienen tendencia a pudrirse en caso de humedad prolongada. A título preventivo, es mejor cortarlas cuando estén marchitas.

Por otra parte, son numerosas las plantas que producen semillas y frutas justo después de la floración. Entonces, durante un buen periodo, no producen más flores. Evitarás esta pausa suprimiendo regularmente las flores marchitas, lo cual impide la formación de semillas y favorece el nacimiento de nuevos botones. Por último, al limpiar tus macetas con cuidado, podrás verificar que tus plantas

El tensiómetro mide la humedad del mantillo y regula el suministro de agua a la balconera.

Cuando gustan las tareas de jardinería, cortar las flores marchitas no es una carga.

no estén enfermas ni invadidas por insectos perjudiciales. Ellas te agradecerán tu esfuerzo estando más bellas todavía.

59

Todas las plantas en imágenes

Agerato
Ageratum houstonianum

Alonsoa
Alonsoa meridionalis

Muraje
Anagallis monellii

Margaritas arbustivas
Argyranthemum frutescens

Estrellada de mar
Asteriscus maritimus

Begonia de porte erguido
Grupo Begonia
tuberhybrida

Begonia colgante Grupo
Begonia tuberhybrida

Bidens, verbena amarilla
Bidens ferulifolia

Braquiscome
Brachyscome multifida

Calceolaria,
zapatillas de la Virgen
Calceolaria integrifolia

Campilla azul
Convolvulus sabatius

Cufea
Cuphea llavea

Clavel de China
Dianthus chinensis

Diascia, reina rosada
Diascia vigilis

Fucsia
Fuchsia (especies
e híbridos diversos)

Gazania
Gazania rigens

Todas las plantas en imágenes

Heliotropo
Heliotropium arborescens

Alegrías de Nueva Guínea
Impatiens × «Nouvelle Guinée»

Lobelia
Lobelia erinus

Lobelia
Lobelia valida

Canastillo,
mastuerzo marítimo
Lobularia maritima

Tabaco ornamental
Nicotiana × sanderae

Onagra
Oenothera fruticosa

Dimorfoteca
Osteospermun ecklonis

Gitanillas,
geranio de hiedra
Pelargonium peltatum

Geranio zonal
Pelargonium × hortorum

Petunia
Petunia × atkinsiana
(= Calibrachoa)

Petunia
Petunia × atkinsiana
«Surfinia»

Salvia azul, salvia perenne
Salvia farinacea

Sanvitalia
Sanvitalia procumbens

Escaveola
Scaevola saligna

Bacopa
Sutera grandiflora

Todas las plantas en imágenes

Tagetes, Cempezúchil
Tagetes tenuifolia

Timofila
Thymophylla tenuiloba

Torenia
Torenia fournieri

Capuchina
Tropaeolum majus

Susana de los ojos negros
Thunbergia alata

Verbena
Verbena (diferentes
especies)

Zinia, hierba del gusano,
pastora
Zinnia angustifolia

Eneldo
Anethum graveolens

Acelga de penca rojas
Beta vulgaris var. cicla

Hiedra terrestre
Glechoma hederacea

Siempreviva amarilla
Helichrysum italicum

Todas las plantas en imágenes

Siempreviva, Nafalión
Helichrysum petiolare

Lavanda
Lavandula angustifolia

Tomate
Lycopersicon esculentum

Mikania, Guaci de cruz
Mikania scandens

Albahaca morada
Ocimum tenuiflorum

Orégano
Origanum vulgare

**Plectranto,
planta del dinero**
Plectranthus forsteri

Romero
Rosmarinus officinalis

Pepino dulce, pera-melón
Solanum muricatum

Tomillo limón
Thymus × citriodorus

Maíz dulce
Zea mays

Índice alfabético

LAW, PUBLIC SAFETY, CORRECTIONS & SECURITY

Bothell, WA • Chicago, IL • Columbus, OH • New York, NY

Image Credits: Cover Photo: George Doyle/Stockbyte/Getty Images.

www.mheonline.com

 **Education**

Copyright © 2012 by The McGraw-Hill Companies, Inc.

Send all inquiries to:
McGraw-Hill Education
130 East Randolph Street, Suite 400
Chicago, IL 60601

ISBN: 978-0-07-661075-4
MHID: 0-07-661075-6

Printed in the United States of America.

 4 5 6 7 8 9 DOH 17 16

CAREER COMPANION
LAW, PUBLIC SAFETY, CORRECTIONS, & SECURITY

CONTENTS

TO THE STUDENT

EXPLORING AND PREPARING FOR A CAREER IN LAW, PUBLIC SAFETY, CORRECTIONS, AND SECURITY

This resource booklet is designed to introduce you to the law, public safety, corrections, and security industry. It will tell you about the variety of jobs in the industry and how to build a career in this field. It will also provide the opportunity to practice the skills that will help you succeed in the industry. Explore the law, public safety, corrections, and security industry and practice the skills presented to help you decide if this industry is right for you.

Finding a job that interests you is the first step in managing your career. To be successful, however, you'll need to explore many job and career possibilities. What if your goals change? What if there is a shift in the labor market or the economy? You may need, or want, to change jobs or even careers. By improving your transferable skills, such as speaking, writing, organizing, planning, and problem solving, you will make yourself a more valuable employee and be able to cope with changes in the labor market. The more transferable skills you develop, the greater your chance of success at any job.

When considering a career in the law, public safety, corrections, and security industry, it is important to understand the realities of the industry. Which jobs have the strongest growth? Which offer good opportunities for advancement? Which jobs align most closely with your own abilities and interests? Are there many jobs available in your area?

Keep these questions in mind as you read Part I of this Career Companion booklet. When you have finished, refer to them again and see how many you can answer. Do the answers make you more or less likely to want to work in this industry? If you feel this industry may be right for you, work your way through the practice questions in Part II. Using real-world situations, they will help you begin preparing for any career in the law, public safety, corrections, and security industry.

EXPLORE

This section of *Career Companion: Law, Public Safety, Corrections, and Security* will introduce you to the law, public safety, corrections, and security industry.

You will explore the following topics:

THE LAW, PUBLIC SAFETY, CORRECTIONS, AND SECURITY INDUSTRY

LAW, PUBLIC SAFETY, CORRECTIONS, AND SECURITY JOBS

BUILDING A CAREER IN LAW, PUBLIC SAFETY, CORRECTIONS, AND SECURITY

EDUCATION AND TRAINING

WORKING IN THE LAW, PUBLIC SAFETY, CORRECTIONS, AND SECURITY INDUSTRY

INDUSTRY TRENDS

CAREER RESOURCES

After exploring this industry, you will be able to answer the following questions:

- What kinds of jobs are available in law, public safety, corrections, and security?
- How can I match my skills and interests with the right job?
- What are the training and education requirements for the job I'm interested in?
- What are some important skills needed to work in this industry?
- What is the work environment like?
- What factors affect trends in the industry?

As you read this book, think about whether the careers described are right for you.

THE LAW, PUBLIC SAFETY, CORRECTIONS, AND SECURITY INDUSTRY

The law, public safety, corrections, and security industry affects nearly every part of our lives. It provides the foundation of law and order that is needed for a healthy society. We rely on the availability and quick response of law enforcement officers, paramedics, and other public safety workers to help and protect us. We count on lawyers and other judicial workers to defend the innocent and bring the guilty to justice.

Think about the many ways law and public safety officials have affected your life. Perhaps there was a fire in your home and firefighters, police, and paramedics came to your aid. Maybe you served on a jury and saw lawyers and judges at work. Maybe you felt reassured when you saw the security guards at your local bank. The men and women of the law, public safety, corrections, and security industry are present throughout the community.

Career Pathways in the Law, Public Safety, Corrections, and Security Industry

A **career cluster** is a grouping of jobs and industries based on common characteristics. A **career pathway** is an area of focus within a career cluster. Each pathway contains a group of careers requiring similar skills as well as similar certifications or education. The law, public safety, corrections, and security career cluster is divided into five main career pathways:

- **Law Enforcement Services**
- **Legal Services**
- **Correction Services**
- **Emergency and Fire Management Services**
- **Security and Protective Services**

Each of these pathways is related. Legal services and correction services relate primarily to the justice system. Emergency and fire management services focus mainly on public safety. Law enforcement services and security and protective services include a combination of justice system and public safety services.

LAW ENFORCEMENT SERVICES

The law enforcement pathway includes employees in a variety of federal, state, county, and city agencies across the United States. Most of these agencies have authority over a certain type of crime or a certain area. People in these occupations enforce the law and protect people in the community. Careers in the law enforcement pathway include police officer, detective, sheriff, animal-control officer, federal marshal, and bailiff.

- Police and patrol officers provide protection from theft and physical harm by patrolling neighborhoods, solving crimes, and building cases against criminals.

- Police detectives gather facts and collect evidence for criminal cases.

- Sheriffs provide county law enforcement services. They are elected by the citizens of their county. Deputy sheriffs work for the county sheriff. They perform duties similar to those of an officer in a city police department.

- US marshals provide protection for federal courts, federal judges, and federal witnesses. They transport federal prisoners and handle goods seized from criminal activities. They may track down escaped prisoners and people who violate their probation and parole.

Applicants for all jobs in this career pathway must meet age, education, and personal background requirements. Nearly all applicants in this pathway must undergo some form of background check. This may include lie-detector tests, drug tests, and criminal record and fingerprint checks. A high school degree or its equivalent is required for most jobs in this pathway. In addition, some police departments and federal agencies require a college degree.

LEGAL SERVICES

There are two main systems of courts in the United States: federal courts and state courts. Both federal and state courts hear civil and criminal cases. Civil law involves disputes, or disagreements, between individuals, such as contract disagreements and divorce.

Occupations in the legal services pathway involve working with the court system. Careers in this pathway include lawyer, judge, paralegal, and legal secretary. All states require lawyers to be members of the bar, or to be licensed. To qualify for the licensing test, an aspiring lawyer must earn an undergraduate degree and a law degree.

Judges are usually lawyers who are elected or appointed to serve in a specific court. Paralegals perform many of the same functions as lawyers, with some restrictions. They are often required to have formal paralegal training through an associate's or bachelor's degree program. Legal secretaries must have knowledge of legal terms and procedures.

CAREER PATHWAYS AND OCCUPATIONS		PROJECTED JOB OPENINGS 2008–2018
Law Enforcement Services	Police and Sheriff's Patrol Officers	227,900
	Transportation Security Officers	71,500
	First-Line Supervisors/Managers of Police and Detectives	50,500
	Criminal Investigators and Special Agents	41,600
	Immigration and Customs Inspectors	41,600
	Police Detectives	41,600
Legal Services	Lawyers	240,400
	Paralegals and Legal Assistants	104,000
	Arbitrators, Mediators, and Conciliators	3,200
Correction Services	Criminal Justice and Law Enforcement Teachers, Postsecondary	552,900
	Correctional Officers and Jailers	143,600
Emergency and Fire Management Services	Business-Continuity Planners	368,300
	Firefighters	152,800
	Police, Fire, and Ambulance Dispatchers	38,400
Security and Protective Services	Security Guards	373,900
	Security Management Specialists	368,300
	Security Managers	297,500
	Loss-Prevention Managers	297,500
	Intelligence Analysts	41,600

Source: *O*NET Occupational Network Database*

CORRECTION SERVICES

The correction services pathway involves the control and treatment of convicted offenders. These careers often involve working with the jail and prison systems. Prisons house convicted offenders who are serving sentences of a year or more. Jails are primarily short-term holding facilities for those who have been arrested or are waiting for a trial. Jails are also used to house convicted offenders who are serving short sentences.

Correctional, parole, and probation officers oversee individuals who have been arrested or convicted of a crime. They also work with people who have been released from jail or prison. Correctional officers guard prisoners and maintain order in jails and prisons. Parole officers help people who have served time in prison return to society. Probation officers work with people who have been spared a jail sentence. In addition to meeting certain educational requirements, applicants for the jobs in this pathway often have specialized training.

EMERGENCY AND FIRE MANAGEMENT SERVICES

Occupations in the emergency and fire management pathway include firefighters, fire protection inspectors, emergency dispatchers, and emergency medical technicians (EMTs). Many positions in this pathway involve working in potentially dangerous situations.

Firefighters provide protection against fires of all kinds. They use heavy equipment, water hoses, and hand tools to fight fires. To become a firefighter, you must pass a written exam along with tests of strength, physical stamina, and agility. Applicants must be at least 18 years old. They must have a high school diploma or the equivalent. Most firefighters go through a long period of on-the-job training. With experience, firefighters may become supervisors, captains, or chiefs.

EMTs and paramedics are specially trained medical technicians. They respond to the scene of accidents or crimes. They provide life-saving emergency care and quick transportation to hospitals. Formal certification and training is required for all EMTs and paramedics.

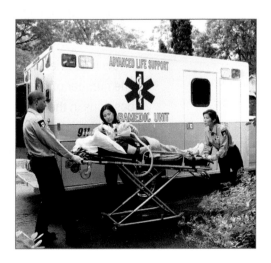

Dispatchers respond to 911 calls and send the appropriate services to an emergency scene. Some emergency dispatchers are trained in emergency medical service. These dispatchers can provide medical assistance over the telephone.

SECURITY AND PROTECTIVE SERVICES

The security and protective services pathway includes a variety of occupations ranging from uniformed security officers (both armed and unarmed) to information security. Careers in this pathway include life guards and ski-patrol personnel. Uniformed security officers are often hired to protect people and property from robberies, fire, and vandalism. They work in public buildings such as museums and banks. They may work for private businesses.

New technology has expanded the security and protective services pathway beyond the traditional uniformed security officers. Computer security specialists and computer forensics specialists focus on the security of digital information. Information security includes careers in IT (information technology) that require expertise in computers and security technology.

Law, Public Safety, Corrections, and Security Industry Outlook

Industry outlook refers to the projected growth or decline in a particular industry. Every year the Bureau of Labor Statistics (BLS) reports on the ten-year outlook for various industries. By 2018 employment in state and local levels of government-related legal, public safety, and corrections occupations is expected to increase about 8 percent over 2008 levels. This is slightly slower than overall growth across all industries, which is projected at about 11 percent. At the federal level, overall 2018 employment is projected to increase about 10 percent over 2008 levels. However, employment for lawyers and judges in the federal government is expected to increase by only 7 to 9 percent.

Employment opportunities in the security area of this industry, including security officers and gaming surveillance officers, are expected to grow slightly faster than average.

A few industries are likely to see growth that is much higher than the average. The number of firefighters is expected to increase 18.9 percent. Government positions in the areas of information security, national security, and federal law enforcement are also expected to grow quickly. Overall, those who specialize in computer security, such as IT information security specialists, will have excellent opportunities.

LAW, PUBLIC SAFETY, CORRECTIONS, AND SECURITY JOB OUTLOOK BY CAREER PATHWAY 2008–2018

PATHWAY	JOB OUTLOOK
Law Enforcement Services	• The number of jobs at the state and local levels is expected to increase about 8 percent. • Rising population levels require increased public safety services. • Opportunities for new hires and advancing workers will result from increased retirements.
Legal Services	• Employment for all types of lawyers is expected to grow about 13 percent. • The number of federal government jobs for lawyers and judicial workers is expected to grow by 7 to 9 percent. • Opportunities exist both in federal courts and in state and local court systems. • Positions for workers who assist lawyers, such as paralegals, are expected to increase by 28 percent.
Correction Services	• The number of openings for correctional officers is expected to grow by 8.3 percent. • The need for social workers, including parole and probation officers, is expected to increase about 24 percent.
Emergency and Fire Management Services	• The number of openings for firefighters is expected to increase by 18.9 percent. • Both forest firefighters and municipal firefighters will have more job opportunities. • The number of emergency medical technician (EMT) and paramedic jobs is expected to increase about 9 percent.
Security and Protective Services	• Growth is expected to be about 14 percent for security guards and gaming surveillance officers. • Opportunities in security management and information security that require computer expertise are expected to grow rapidly. • As the gaming industry experiences moderate growth, gaming surveillance and casino security guards will have more opportunities.

Source: US Department of Labor, *Career Guide to Industries 2010–2011* and *O*NET Occupational Network Database*

LAW, PUBLIC SAFETY, CORRECTIONS, AND SECURITY JOBS

You can find jobs at all skill levels that suit a variety of interests in the law, public safety, corrections, and security industry. People interested in public safety can become a police officer, dispatcher, emergency medical technician, or firefighter. Those interested in other pathways in this cluster can become a lawyer, paralegal, corrections officer, or security guard. Here are some common industry jobs and the skills they require.

CAREER PATHWAY ▶ Law Enforcement Services

POLICE PATROL OFFICER

Police patrol officers protect the lives and property of citizens. They respond to emergency calls and make sure people obey laws. They maintain order in public areas. Officers in small towns patrol their community and respond to accidents, fires, and other problems. Officers in larger cities are often assigned to a small area within the city. They usually spend several hours a week patrolling by foot, on horseback, or by car.

Some officers work in a specialized unit, such as a special weapons and tactics (SWAT) team. These officers respond to high-risk situations, such as hostage crises or riots.

Special Skills Police patrol officers need excellent people skills and communication skills. They need a good understanding of local, state, and federal laws and procedures. Police officers must be able to work in stressful situations and to handle weapons and potentially dangerous suspects safely. They must meet the police department's entrance requirements, which usually include good vision and hearing, physical agility, and clean criminal and driving records.

TRANSPORTATION SECURITY OFFICER

Transportation security officers inspect baggage and cargo before they are loaded on an airplane. They screen passengers and search for dangerous objects or weapons that passengers might be carrying. Transportation security officers may detain people who behave suspiciously, identify suspicious packages, and test baggage for explosives.

Special Skills Transportation security officers must be familiar with the security policies and procedures at an airport. They should be able to focus on details. They should also have good reasoning ability and be able to accurately identify suspicious people or items.

FORENSIC SCIENCE TECHNICIAN

Forensic science technicians help solve crimes. They collect evidence from crime scenes. Then they use science to analyze the evidence in a criminal investigation. These technicians work in a number of specialties.

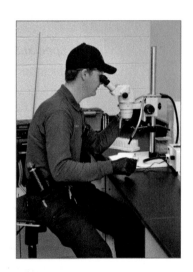

Ballistics technicians, for example, examine bullets found in victims or at crime scenes. Technicians who specialize in chemistry may analyze a chip of paint from an automobile. They may analyze hair, dirt, blood, and biological tissues and fluids found at crime scenes. Other technicians specialize in analyzing handwriting or fingerprints and footprints.

Special Skills Forensic science technicians work closely with FBI agents and local police departments, so they must work well with people. They must be mentally prepared to go to crime scenes and witness the effects of violent acts. They must have a thorough understanding of lab procedures and instruments, and they must know how to handle evidence.

CAREER PATHWAY ▶ Legal Services

LAWYER

Lawyers (who are sometimes called attorneys) research, interpret, and apply the law. They prepare legal documents, such as wills and contracts. They advise their clients on legal matters. They represent their clients in court. Lawyers usually specialize in an area of the law, such as criminal, civil, or corporate law.

Criminal defense attorneys, for example, defend clients who have been charged with a crime. Other lawyers specialize in civil law, which involves noncriminal disputes between individuals or organizations.

Special Skills Effective lawyers have excellent written and oral communication skills. They need to organize their thoughts well and speak clearly. They must be able to persuade and negotiate. Lawyers must have excellent reading and analytical skills.

PARALEGAL

Paralegals, and other legal assistants, perform many of the same tasks that lawyers perform. They assist lawyers with hearings, trials, meetings, and depositions. A deposition is an oral statement that is made under oath. Paralegals track down public documents, records, and previous legal decisions relevant to a case. They organize information and prepare written reports. Paralegals also help prepare legal documents, such as wills and contracts.

Special Skills Because paralegals frequently research and write legal documents, they must have excellent reading and writing skills. They must be familiar with the important reference works and cases in their field. They must know how to use legal libraries and databases. Paralegals must be organized, helpful, and good at working with both lawyers and clients.

ARBITRATOR, MEDIATOR, AND CONCILIATOR

Arbitrators, mediators, and conciliators help resolve conflicts and negotiate solutions to problems. They do this outside the court system. They often organize meetings between the parties involved in a dispute. They try to clarify the problem and help each party understand the concerns and needs of the other party. The goal of mediation is to arrive at a solution that both sides can agree to. Arbitrators, mediators, and conciliators have to understand the laws that relate to a situation and determine possible solutions based on those laws.

Special Skills Arbitrators, mediators, and conciliators must be able to listen to people and communicate well with them. Since they are often involved in conflict resolution, they need to be sensitive to the needs and concerns of others. A thorough understanding of how laws are applied is important. They must have strong reading and writing skills. They also need to have excellent problem-solving and decision-making skills.

CAREER PATHWAY ▶ Correction Services

CORRECTIONAL OFFICER

Correctional officers protect communities by guarding inmates in prisons and jails. They may work at high-security, medium-security, or low-security prisons.

Correctional officers monitor activities in various areas of prisons. They make sure that inmates obey the rules and remain orderly. They search cells for weapons and settle conflicts between inmates. They inspect the building for signs of escape attempts. Correctional officers escort inmates from their cells to the dining areas, classrooms, religious worship areas, and work areas. Some correctional officers guard prisoners who have jobs in the community as they go to and from their work. They may escort prisoners to and from court.

Special Skills Correctional officers must be in good physical condition. They must have an understanding of the laws related to prisons and prisoners' rights. They must follow the security and safety procedures outlined by their employers and be willing to risk injury to maintain order. Correctional officers need good judgment, common sense, and the ability to communicate well.

PROBATION OFFICER

Probation officers, parole officers, and other correctional specialists help people who have been convicted of a crime. Parole officers help people return to society after serving time in prison. Probation officers monitor people who have been sentenced to probation instead of prison. Both parole and probation officers make sure clients obey the law and the terms of their paroles or probations. These officers help ex-offenders by advising them on education, job, financial, and housing issues and by directing them to community services. Officers keep written records of the ex-offenders' behavior and progress.

Special Skills Parole and probation officers must have good communication skills and a desire to help people. Because they deal with many social problems, they need to be tolerant and understanding, but also firm. They should be able to resist becoming depressed or overwhelmed. They need a thorough knowledge of the various social services available to ex-offenders.

Emergency and Fire Management Services

FIREFIGHTER

Firefighters respond to fires. They rescue victims from burning buildings, connect hoses to fire hydrants, climb ladders and position hoses, and ventilate smoke-filled buildings. Firefighters put out most fires by spraying water, but some chemical fires must be put out with special extinguishing chemicals. In cities, firefighters obtain water by attaching fire hoses to hydrants. In rural or uninhabited areas, they use rivers, ponds, or large tanker trucks that carry water to the scene of fires. Some firefighters specialize in putting out forest fires. Many firefighters are trained to administer first aid to victims of automobile accidents, heart attacks, drowning, and other emergencies.

Special Skills Firefighters must be physically strong and in excellent physical condition. They must not be afraid to climb to great heights. They must be able to stay calm in dangerous situations and have good communication skills. To become a firefighter, applicants often have to pass a written test, an oral interview, a physical-abilities test, a medical evaluation, and a background investigation.

EMERGENCY MANAGEMENT SPECIALIST

Emergency management specialists respond to crises such as natural disasters and hostage situations. They plan for emergencies and carry out those plans when needed. They train others so that responses to emergencies can be accomplished quickly and effectively.

In addition, emergency management specialists work closely with government officials. They stay informed on laws and regulations that relate to disaster response. They may work to make sure that a state or city provides enough money so emergency plans can be carried out.

Special Skills Emergency management specialists need to have good written and oral communication skills. They must have strong problem-solving skills, a logical mind, and the ability to choose a course of action from a variety of possible plans. They must be able to act calmly and think clearly in a crisis situation.

CAREER PATHWAY # Security and Protective Services

SECURITY GUARD

Security guards protect people and property. They keep buildings and their contents safe from robberies, vandalism, and other illegal activity. Guards work in banks, museums, government offices, retail stores, factories, and offices. At department stores, guards primarily check for theft. They patrol the sales floor or monitor sales areas from a control room. If necessary, they detain thieves until the police arrive. Guards working in hospitals, banks, and office buildings protect property, staff, and customers by monitoring security camera videos and patrolling the grounds. Guards who work at stadiums and universities maintain crowd control, supervise parking, and direct traffic. Some security guards work at loading platforms in warehouses, factories, railroad stations, and ports.

Special Skills Security guards must stay alert and be willing to sit or stand for long periods of time. They must be able to work alone. They often work unusual hours, including nights and weekends. Guards should be in good physical condition and have good vision. They need to be able to spot signs of trouble and deal with a variety of problems, including potential violence.

SECURITY MANAGEMENT SPECIALIST

Security management specialists are involved in all aspects of security for organizations. They may work for hospitals, banks, casinos, or other businesses where a high level of security is required. These security specialists design security systems and make sure they are installed and used correctly. They may inspect and assess existing security procedures and recommend improvements. It is very important that security management specialists stay up-to-date on new security technology.

Special Skills Rapid developments in computer technology and sophisticated security systems mean that a background in computer science may be necessary for many security management specialists. Strong problem-solving skills and the ability to think clearly and logically are important. In addition, security management specialists must be able to develop solutions to problems and apply these solutions to real situations.

CHAPTER 3

BUILDING A CAREER IN LAW, PUBLIC SAFETY, CORRECTIONS, AND SECURITY

Once you have found a field that interests you, look ahead and consider your career path. This path is made up of the job experiences and the career moves that lead you toward your career goal. You may take several steps before reaching your ultimate goal. You will likely spend time in an entry-level position. This will help you gain the professional experience necessary to move ahead in your career.

For example, a lawyer's career path begins with four years of undergraduate study followed by three years of law school. During the summer, most law students work as interns. Upon graduation, they must pass a state bar examination. Most new lawyers join law firms. After several years of experience, lawyers may become partners in law firms, or they may start their own firms.

Don't worry if you change your mind about your career path. This happens to many people. It often takes time to find the right path. You can always change your career path regardless of where you are in your chosen profession.

Evaluating Career Choices

Choosing a career is challenging. Now is a good time to start thinking about what kind of career path you would like to follow. A well-chosen career can bring satisfaction and success in life.

Self-knowledge is the key to making wise career choices. Friends, teachers, and family members may offer helpful suggestions for potential careers. However, you are ultimately in charge of making your own career decisions.

Consider your personality, interests, aptitudes, and values when choosing a career. Think about why you chose to read this book. Of the many industries in which you could work, why does law, public safety, corrections, and security appeal to you?

You might feel that your personality, the way you think and behave, is well suited to this industry. If you are perceptive, hardworking, and interested in helping people, then a career in law, public safety, corrections, and security may be a good choice.

You should also allow your interests to influence your career decisions. What activities do you enjoy? Volunteering for political campaigns, computer programming, and public speaking can build skills related to careers in law, public safety, corrections, and security. If you enjoy activities that are physically challenging and require endurance, a physically demanding job such as police officer or firefighter might be a good choice.

In some cases, your aptitude, or ability in a certain area, will shape your career goals. A talent for observing and understanding people's behavior would be an asset in a career in law enforcement. Physical strength and agility could help you succeed as a firefighter. However, aptitude is not the same as interest. You might have strong artistic abilities, for example, but choose a career that uses other skills.

Values are another factor to consider when selecting a career. Values are the principles and beliefs that you live by. You might value responsibility, compassion, security, courage, recognition, independence, leadership, or creativity. Your values will shape all areas of your life, from your long-term goals to the lifestyle you lead. For example, if you value family time, you might seek a job that allows for flextime and provides good vacation benefits.

SUCCESS IN THE LAW, PUBLIC SAFETY, CORRECTIONS, AND SECURITY CAREER CLUSTER

The career opportunities in the law, public safety, corrections, and security industry are broad enough to accommodate workers with a variety of personality traits, interests, aptitudes, and values.

Your satisfaction working in this industry will depend on how well you match yourself to a particular job. If you are still uncertain about your desired career path, there are resources that can help. You can take self-assessment tests to find a career that matches your strengths. Part-time or temporary work can also help you discover your aptitudes and interests.

The careers profiled in this book represent just some of the jobs available in the law, public safety, corrections, and security industry. There are too many jobs to list in just one book. Also, the workplace is constantly changing. Opportunities in traditional fields continue to expand, and new opportunities are constantly arising.

Learning about the range of job opportunities available to you will give you an advantage when you begin your job search. Developing workplace skills and learning about aspects of the law, public safety, corrections, and security industry will also help you. As you make your career choices, think positively, keeping in mind your best attributes. Set ambitious but realistic goals and keep an open mind about opportunities that may arise.

WORKING WITH DATA, PEOPLE, AND THINGS

Most careers offer opportunities to work with a combination of data, people, and things. Working with data involves the evaluation of information. A job that focuses on people will be based on human relationships. Working with things involves using objects, such as tools, equipment, and machines. Most jobs focus mainly on one of these areas. Legal assistants, for example, work mainly with data. Probation officers work primarily with people. Firefighters work mostly with things.

CAREERS THAT INVOLVE WORKING WITH DATA

Working with data means working with words, ideas, concepts, and numbers. Examples of working with data include preparing financial statements and drawing up budgets, researching laws and previous decisions to prepare for court cases, and putting together clues to solve crimes.

Jobs that focus on data are often found in fire departments, police departments, and law firms. Fire investigators may need to go to fires to determine how the blaze started. This requires conducting research, running tests, and collecting and analyzing data. Crime laboratory technicians in police departments perform calculations and make predictions based on data. Security specialists may analyze a security system to make sure it is effective. Judges need to consider complex ideas, documents, and legal principles when making their decisions.

Some managers in law enforcement need to work with data. A state-trooper supervisor, for instance, will study spreadsheets that display crime rates to determine whether current methods of crime prevention are efficient and cost-effective.

Are you good with words and numbers? Do you enjoy applying scientific and mathematical principles to everyday situations? Do you grasp new concepts quickly? Do people say that you think logically? If so, you may want to consider a career that focuses on working with data.

CAREERS THAT INVOLVE WORKING WITH PEOPLE

Many law, public safety, corrections, and security jobs focus on working with people. Examples of working with people include training new police recruits, mediating conflicts, negotiating with hostage-takers, and counseling a prisoner on probation. All of these activities require strong communication skills.

In addition, many of the jobs in this industry involve working closely with others. Paramedics, for example, must supervise and lead teams of EMTs. Firefighters must work together effectively. Police officers, lawyers, and judges have to communicate with one another and with people from many different backgrounds.

People who enjoy working with other people are generally outgoing. To decide if you're a "people person," ask yourself a few questions. Do you place great emphasis on your friendships? Do you spend your spare time socializing with friends or family? Are you good at judging the motivations and feelings of others? If so, you'll probably enjoy a job that allows for frequent interaction with others.

CAREERS THAT INVOLVE WORKING WITH THINGS

All careers in law, public safety, corrections, and security involve working with things. Examples of things that people in this industry work with include crime scene evidence, crime laboratory equipment, firearms and weapons, and other kinds of equipment, such as breathalyzers and radar speed detectors. Firefighters spend time each day working with and maintaining ladders, hoses, fire trucks, and other equipment. Police, corrections, and security officers deal with a wide range of equipment on their job.

Think about how you choose to spend your spare time. Do you enjoy building, assembling, or repairing things? Are you curious about how machines like cars or computers actually work? Do you prefer to work with your hands? If so, you're probably well suited for working with things.

DATA, PEOPLE, AND THINGS IN LAW, PUBLIC SAFETY, CORRECTIONS, AND SECURITY

Whatever career in law, public safety, corrections, and security you choose, you're likely to spend some time working with data, people, and things. Choosing a job that matches what you like to do will make you a better employee and a happier person.

How can you find a job that best suits your strengths? One way is by browsing the Dictionary of Occupational Titles (www.occupationalinfo.org). This resource lists a wide range of jobs. Each job has a nine-digit code that identifies and describes it. The fourth, fifth, and sixth digits show how much each job involves working with data, people, and things, respectively. The lower the number, the more complex the particular type of work. For example, a security guard's code is 189.167-034. This job involves providing security for businesses and public places. The digits 1, 6, and 7 mean complex work with data, less complex work with people, and much simpler work with things. A firefighter's code is 373.364-010. The digits 3, 6, and 4 mean that the job involves complex work with data, less complex work with people, and moderately complex work with things.

Finding Employment

Finding a job is seldom easy, but finding a job in a new career field can be even harder. Whether you have a job but are considering a career change or are unemployed, now is a good time to explore new careers and make yourself more valuable to employers.

CHANGING CAREERS

Many people jump from one career right into another. They may feel that their job does not match their skills or interests. They may believe the job does not offer enough room to advance. A new career can offer different opportunities.

The best time to think about a new career is when you are already employed. While you have a job, there is less pressure to find a new job right away. Investigate which career fields have good opportunities in the area where you live. Think about your current job. What aspects of it do you enjoy? Which other careers involve similar tasks?

If you find a job that you would like to pursue, spend time investigating the qualifications required. You might speak to someone who works in the industry. Learn as much as you can to ensure the career cluster is right for you.

Look for ways you can gain experience that will help you in your search. If the new career involves working with people, volunteer for tasks in which you will interact with people. You should also spend time creating a résumé. Use print and online resources to learn how to create the résumé that best highlights your qualifications. Highlight the skills that are most relevant to the jobs you will apply for.

You should also spend time networking, or reaching out to people who can help in your job search. This may include family, friends, or colleagues from current or former jobs. Make an effort to meet new people to expand your network. One good way to do this is to use online networking sites.

UNEMPLOYMENT

Being unemployed can be a difficult time, but it also brings new opportunities. Millions of people are unemployed at any time, so there is no shame in being unemployed. If you find yourself unemployed, apply for unemployment benefits. Benefits are given only after you are approved, so be sure to apply right away.

Make the most of your time while you are unemployed. Work on your résumé. Expand your network. Try to stick to a daily schedule. For example, you might shower and dress as if going to work and then spend the morning crafting your résumé or searching for jobs. Rather than spending every waking hour looking for work, set aside some time for leisure activities.

Consider finding a freelance or part-time job that can help you gain new skills and earn more money while you search. You might also take a class that teaches skills useful in a new career.

EDUCATION AND TRAINING

All jobs in law, public safety, corrections, and security require job-specific knowledge and skills. Some require specialized on-the-job training. Police officers, for example, receive intensive job training through department-run academies. Other jobs require at least some higher education. Paralegals often need to complete a two-year program at a community college. Federal agents must have a four-year college degree plus specialized training. Lawyers need four years of college and three years of law school. Criminologists and forensic scientists need PhDs to prepare them to conduct independent research.

Training and Education for Law, Public Safety, Corrections, and Security

The level of training and education needed varies by career. Jobs can be categorized into three groups—those requiring little training, those requiring some training, and those requiring advanced training.

JOBS REQUIRING LITTLE TRAINING

Most jobs in the industry require at least some formal training. However, there are some jobs in this industry that require less than the average amount of training. Depending on the job, this training can be obtained at a technical school, a community college, or on the job. These jobs include security guards, prison guards, police dispatchers, and 911 operators.

JOBS REQUIRING SOME TRAINING

Many jobs in this industry require a moderate level of education and training. For example, police officers, firefighters, and correctional officers complete a formal training program as well as on-the-job training. Police officers study federal, state, and local laws. They participate in hours of physical and practical training each day. Candidates run, lift weights, and increase their endurance. They learn how to handle firearms and cope with dangerous situations. Firefighters learn the science of fires and the operation of fire equipment. They practice search-and-rescue techniques and receive EMT training. You don't need a college degree to enter many careers in this industry. However, a college degree improves your opportunities for promotion and higher pay.

For other jobs in this industry, certification is required. For example, you can become certified as an EMT, a firefighter, or a paralegal. Some of these jobs may require ongoing education.

JOBS REQUIRING ADVANCED TRAINING

Some careers in this industry require a high level of training and education. This education is often in the form of a master's or a doctoral degree. A master's degree is granted after a one- to two-year program of study beyond the bachelor's degree level at a university or college. A doctoral degree is an advanced degree. A doctoral degree signifies that an individual is an expert in a particular field. Doctoral students must write and defend an original scholarly paper, called a dissertation, that studies an important idea in detail.

People who work in the science of crime and rehabilitation generally need postgraduate degrees. Criminologists, forensic scientists, and psychologists all need master's degrees, and many of these professionals hold doctoral degrees. Criminologists, for instance, usually hold master's and doctoral degrees in fields such as clinical psychology, sociology, and criminology. Parole and probation officers may benefit from pursuing master's degrees in psychology, sociology, or other related fields.

Lawyers must earn both a bachelor's degree and a juris doctor (JD) degree. In college, aspiring lawyers take courses in English, history, political science, economics, foreign language, computer science, and social sciences. The law school application process is very selective. Admission is based on college grades and scores on the Law School Admission Test (LSAT). Law school generally lasts three years. Lawyers must pass the bar exam before they are accepted into the bar. The bar is the organization of lawyers in a state. The bar exam varies from state to state, but it is usually a two-day test.

TRAINING REQUIRED FOR LAW, PUBLIC SAFETY, CORRECTIONS, AND SECURITY JOBS	
Jobs Requiring Little to No Training	
Animal Control Workers	Security Guards
Bailiffs	Transportation Security Officers
Parking Enforcement Workers	
Police, Fire, and Ambulance Dispatchers	
Jobs Requiring Some Training or Education	
Correctional Officers and Jailers	Police Patrol Officers
Firefighters	Private Detectives and Investigators
Paralegals and Legal Assistants	Sheriffs and Deputy Sheriffs
Police Detectives	
Jobs Requiring Advanced Training or Education	
Arbitrators, Mediators, and Conciliators	Judges and Magistrates
Forensic Science Technicians	Law Clerks
Intelligence Analysts	Lawyers
	Security Management Specialists

Pre-Employment Training

Pre-employment training for positions in law, public safety, corrections, and security may involve completing one or more of the following:

- an apprenticeship or internship

- a certification or specialized program at an academy or community college

- a bachelor's, master's, or doctoral degree program at a college or university

Before seeking formal training, look for ways to get on-the-job training. Some employers provide such training for entry-level employees.

APPRENTICESHIPS

An apprenticeship is a way to gain real-life work experience. In an apprenticeship, an inexperienced worker learns a trade by working alongside an expert worker. Some apprenticeships last as long as four or five years, and the student earns little pay. However, workers who have completed these programs are often well respected and well paid.

Fire departments sometimes offer apprenticeship programs, which can last up to five years. These programs combine formal, technical instruction with on-the-job training under the supervision of experienced firefighters. The US Department of Labor's Office of Apprenticeship (http://oa.doleta.gov/) is an excellent source of leads for apprenticeship opportunities.

POSTSECONDARY EDUCATION

Most skilled and professional workers in the law, public safety, corrections, and security industry have completed at least some postsecondary education. Postsecondary education refers to study done after high school. Most people seek postsecondary education at universities, technical schools, or community colleges.

Police officers with a college degree can advance to higher ranks more quickly than their coworkers without degrees. As a firefighter, community college courses in fire science are helpful, but a two- or four-year degree in fire science or fire engineering will give you more career mobility. A bachelor's degree in fire science or public administration is often necessary to advance beyond the level of battalion chief.

Some other jobs in this industry require postsecondary education. Paramedics, for example, are often required to complete a two-year degree before taking the certification exam to become a paramedic. Many paramedics later obtain additional education to become a nurse, physician's assistant, or doctor.

INTERNSHIPS

An internship is an opportunity to gain practical experience in a field. Internships are usually shorter than apprenticeships. They may offer the opportunity to learn about various departments in a company. An intern often receives little or no pay. However, completing an internship can improve your chances of getting a job. Many companies post information about internship opportunities on their websites.

TECHNICAL SCHOOLS

If you're interested in a position that requires training, a technical school is a promising option. A technical school offers skills-oriented programs. It might offer courses in computer repair or information technology that would help prepare you for a career in the law, public safety, corrections, and security industry.

Most paralegals complete two- or four-year programs in paralegal studies. The American Bar Association (ABA) approves hundreds of these programs across the country. The National Association of Legal Assistants (NALA) provides several ways to become a certified paralegal. Most paralegals must be recertified on a regular basis.

Federal law enforcement agencies usually require a college degree and a passing grade on an entrance exam. In some agencies, significant on-the-job experience can substitute for a college degree. Like police officers, candidates then undergo formal training at an academy. This training is followed by on-the-job training.

Parole officers, probation officers, and other correctional treatment specialists must obtain postsecondary education. This is usually in the form of a bachelor's degree in social work, psychology, or criminal justice. Those who want to advance in their careers often go on to obtain a master's degree, which usually involves two years of additional study.

Before choosing an educational program, make sure that the program will prepare you for the job you want. Consider the length of the program. Check that the program is nationally accredited. Take into consideration a school's reputation in the field. Another important factor is cost. Contact the financial aid office of the schools that interest you to find out how to apply for financial aid.

POSTGRADUATE EDUCATION

Postgraduate education, or graduate school, follows the completion of a bachelor's degree. Most people who seek postgraduate education enroll in master's or doctoral degree programs.

Many upper-level law enforcement officers have completed a postgraduate education. Most parole and probation officers, criminologists, and forensic scientists have advanced degrees. As jobs in law enforcement become more competitive, an increasing number of law enforcement agencies prefer candidates who have at least a four-year degree. A master's or doctoral degree may give a job candidate an extra edge.

Many professionals put off graduate school. Instead, they take an entry-level job in their field after completing their undergraduate degree. This enables them to gain experience and perhaps qualify for company-sponsored tuition assistance programs.

When admitting students for master's and doctoral degree programs, universities consider candidates' academic record. Work experience is sometimes considered. In most cases, admission is very selective. Those who wish to earn postgraduate degrees must have strong academic backgrounds.

On-the-Job Training

On-the-job training is on-site instruction in how to perform a particular job. If you're seeking a job in law, public safety, corrections, and security, your employer will most likely conduct some level of on-the-job training.

On-the-job training brings several benefits. First, this type of training is usually paid. However, even unpaid training provides you with knowledge and skills. Second, the training is tailored to the job. By the time you complete your training, you'll probably feel comfortable in your new position.

TYPES OF ON-THE-JOB TRAINING

Jobs that offer on-the-job training are available in most law, public safety, corrections, and security pathways. In addition to completing a formal training program at a law enforcement academy, law enforcement officers participate in on-the-job training. During this time, they put to use all the education and training they received at the academy.

Security guards and correctional officers rely on on-the-job training to learn real-life applications of the procedures they practiced during their formal training.

Even lawyers need on-the-job training. A lawyer just out of law school who takes a position in an attorney general's office will have to become familiar with the practices and procedures of that job and that agency.

Many paid apprenticeships qualify as on-the job training. This is especially true if they are sponsored by the company employing the apprentice. Such apprenticeships may require that the apprentice work at the sponsor company for a certain length of time after completing the apprenticeship.

Job and Workplace Skills

When considering job candidates, employers look for both job-specific skills and general workplace skills. Job-specific skills are the skills necessary to do a particular job. They may include preparing a legal form or attaching a fire hose to a tanker truck. General workplace skills are skills that can be used in a variety of jobs.

INDUSTRY SKILL STANDARDS

Many positions in law and public safety require applicants to meet specific skill standards. This may include licensing, certification, or completion of a particular training program. Some positions, including police officer, federal agent, firefighter, and security guard, require applicants to pass a written examination as well as a physical test.

Some positions require certification in addition to employer training programs. For example, EMTs and paramedics must be formally certified and registered before they can work. Extensive coursework and field experience are required. In some states, security guards must be certified before they can legally work. Paralegals can become certified through a variety of exams and certification programs. Often employees must be regularly recertified.

CORE SKILLS

Core skills differ from academic or job-specific skills. They are learned both inside and outside the classroom. They are transferable from job to job. Developing these skills will not only prepare you for jobs in the law, public safety, corrections, and security industry but for all jobs.

Communication Skills In the law, public safety, corrections, and security industry, effective verbal communication is of the utmost importance. Police officers and firefighters must be able to communicate clearly so they can help victims of crimes and disasters. Communication skills are also important when testifying in court and when communicating with colleagues.

Listening Skills Listening skills are necessary for police detectives who question citizens and must get the facts straight. Lawyers need to be able to listen carefully to their clients and to judges. Emergency workers need to listen for details about a situation from a variety of sources.

Problem-Solving Skills Employers value workers who can spot problems and take action to find solutions. Solving problems requires creativity and confidence. A correctional officer might be called on to solve conflicts between inmates. Detectives use problem-solving skills to solve crimes. EMTs use problem-solving skills to assess a patient's injuries and begin treatment.

Technology Skills Most jobs in law and public safety involve the use of computer technology. Many police officers use computers in their cars to guide them from one call to another. In courtrooms, judges use computers to access the criminal and driving records of defendants. Legal secretaries use computers to produce daily work logs. Security specialists may need extensive computer knowledge to install and operate complex security systems.

Decision-Making Skills Judges, law enforcement officers, and emergency workers frequently need to make important decisions. They must be able to gather and analyze information rapidly. They have to think clearly under pressure. The decisions they make have a direct effect on people's lives. A parole officer's decisions might make the difference between a dangerous criminal staying in prison and the prisoner being set free.

Organizing and Planning Skills Planning requires the ability to set goals and identify the steps leading to these goals. Judges and lawyers must manage their court schedules and large amounts of casework. Police chiefs must organize their staff and keep track of the cases in their department. Paralegals must perform research and organize it into briefs and other legal documents.

Teamwork Skills Teamwork is key in many law, public safety, corrections, and security careers. At an accident scene, for example, police officers, EMTs, and firefighters all work together to help victims. Similarly, judges, lawyers, and parole officers work closely together. Teamwork is essential for members of federal, state, and local law enforcement agencies, who may need to work together to solve a crime.

Social Skills Some jobs do not require much social interaction with coworkers. However, social interaction makes for a more enjoyable and productive workplace. In this industry, workers interact with individuals from various levels of their organization. They can use these opportunities to learn from others.

Adaptability Skills Job requirements, work environments, and safety procedures are constantly changing along with technological innovations and changes in the law. The ability to learn new technologies and procedures is essential in today's workplace and job market.

CHAPTER 5

WORKING IN THE LAW, PUBLIC SAFETY, CORRECTIONS, AND SECURITY INDUSTRY

When choosing a career path, it is important to know what it is like to work in the industry. Understanding the work environment, hazards, and benefits of a job can help you make informed decisions.

Work Environment

Work environment refers to factors that affect workers' health and satisfaction on the job. These include the physical surroundings and the working hours. They also include the physical activities required to perform the job.

PHYSICAL ENVIRONMENT

The physical work environment in this industry varies by job.

Professionals such as lawyers, judges, and paralegals who spend a majority of their time in offices or courtrooms enjoy a pleasant work environment.

Correctional officers often work in modern buildings, but their work environment is at times unpleasant. Prisons are often noisy. Because of the safety hazards in prisons, officers must follow complicated security procedures.

Security officers often stand or walk for most of their shift. Security officers may work in museums, banks, casinos, concert venues, stadiums, or parks.

Police officers, firefighters, and EMTs spend much of their time outside, patrolling or working at crime scenes and accidents. Firefighters must withstand extreme heat. They risk inhaling smoke, falling from ladders or buildings, or receiving severe burns. Police officers and other law enforcement professionals may risk injury when pursuing a fleeing suspect by foot or by car.

WORKING CONDITIONS IN LAW, PUBLIC SAFETY, CORRECTIONS, AND SECURITY

Law Enforcement Services

- Officers may spend most of their shift patrolling by car or on foot.
- Officers may face dangerous and even life-threatening situations.
- Detectives and investigators spend some time in an office and some time in the field.
- Surveillance may require sitting or standing for long periods of time; it may require working in the early mornings, late nights, and weekends.

Legal Services

- Most legal professionals work in clean, comfortable offices or courtrooms.
- Some workers suffer from repetitive stress injuries and eyestrain.
- Most employees work long hours.
- Jobs are often demanding and stressful.

Correction Services

- Correctional officers often handle dangerous situations that arise between inmates.
- Correctional officers may have to contend with high noise levels.
- Parole and probation officers spend time in prisons and courtrooms. They may encounter dangerous and angry people. Some have to carry a weapon.

Emergency and Fire Management Services

- Firefighters are at high risk of injury or death from exposure to fire, smoke, and falling debris.
- Firefighters work irregular hours, including overnight shifts, and they must be ready to respond to a call at any minute.
- EMTs and paramedics risk exposure to communicable diseases such as AIDS and hepatitis-B.
- A typical workweek for EMTs is 40 to 60 hours; work on weekends and holidays may be required.

Security and Protective Services

- Gaming surveillance officers work in noisy casinos; sometimes they must deal with unpleasant or angry people.
- Security officers work in the field, in control rooms, and in guard shacks.
- Security officers may have to sit or stand for long periods of time.

Source: US Department of Labor, *Career Guide to Industries 2010–2011* and *O*NET*

WORK HOURS

The work hours for careers in this industry vary greatly. While some careers follow a typical 9-to-5 schedule, many others require shift work or irregular hours to ensure the safety of the population.

Law Enforcement Services   Because citizens need law enforcement officers 365 days a year, 24 hours a day, shift work is vital in this pathway. Shift work divides the day into blocks of time, often eight hours. Shift work allows citizens to have police services available around the clock. It also gives officers the possibility of selecting the hours they want to work. Some shifts are permanent, while others rotate on a weekly, biweekly, or monthly basis.

Legal Services   Lawyers, judges, paralegals, and mediators typically work eight to 12 hours a day. They often work overtime to meet the needs of their clients. If several court cases are pending, lawyers and paralegals must work overtime to prepare for court. They often meet with clients in the late afternoon or early evening.

Correction Services   Workers in this pathway have a variety of work hours and situations. Corrections officers rely on shifts to make sure prison inmates are supervised at all times. Parole and probation officers typically work eight to 12 hours a day.

Emergency and Fire Management Services   Like the law enforcement pathway, shift work in emergency and fire management is common. It allows citizens to have fire and emergency medical services available around the clock. Firefighters often work 24-hour shifts with two days off between shifts. They may work longer when needed for emergency situations.

Security and Protective Services   Security professionals, such as security officers and gaming surveillance officers, work shifts to make sure a business or building is secure at all times. These shifts are typically about eight hours long. Part-time work is common in this pathway.

ESSENTIAL PHYSICAL ACTIVITIES

Workers must be in good physical condition for many law, public safety, corrections, and security jobs. Law enforcement officers must be able to run and to climb fences and other barriers. They must have enough endurance for a foot pursuit. They often need to stand or walk for long periods of time. Firefighters have to climb ladders, fences, and other structures. They must carry heavy firefighting equipment up many flights of stairs and wear gear that may weigh up to 40 pounds.

Good vision is a must for many workers in this pathway. Accurate vision is needed to fire weapons, see at night, and write and read reports and instructions. Glasses and contact lenses are usually permitted to correct vision problems.

Hazards and Environmental Dangers

Because accidents can happen on any job, safety must be a priority. The federal government protects workers by creating workplace safety standards and laws. These rules help prevent accidents and ensure that accident victims are offered assistance.

INJURIES AND ILLNESSES

Most on-the-job impairments are either occupational injuries or occupational illnesses. An occupational injury is any injury that occurs at work. Such injuries include cuts, fractures, and sprains. An occupational illness is an illness caused by on-the-job exposure to harmful substances. Illnesses include rashes and skin diseases, respiratory problems, or poisoning.

Many law, public safety, corrections, and security jobs involve operating heavy equipment and entering dangerous situations. Firefighters must enter burning buildings. They may be exposed to hazardous chemicals, fumes, or construction materials. Correctional and police officers may encounter dangerous situations, including those involving weapons. Security professionals also may encounter life-threatening situations on the job. Armored car guards carry weapons and wear bulletproof vests. Gaming surveillance officers, who make sure casinos are secure, have a high rate of injury. Proper training and common sense are necessary for handling dangerous situations.

Another job hazard is injury to the eyes. Eye protection is necessary if workers come in contact with sharp objects or are exposed to chemicals. Showers and eye baths must be available to workers who are at risk for eye damage. Police officers use eye baths if they get pepper spray in their eyes while spraying a suspect.

Workers may be exposed to chemicals that are dangerous to touch or breathe. Even dust in the air can harm the lungs and prevent normal breathing. Safety shoes, gloves, and respirators must be available to all workers who are exposed to dangerous substances.

Employees, such as paralegals, who work at computers for long periods of time may suffer from repetitive-stress injuries and eyestrain. Repetitive-stress injuries (RSIs) can develop when the same motions are performed over and over. One of the most common RSIs is carpal tunnel syndrome, a swelling of tendons in the wrist. This injury can result from frequently repeated tasks such as typing. Eyestrain can develop from reading printed material or using a computer.

RATES OF WORK-RELATED INJURIES AND ILLNESSES IN THE LAW, PUBLIC SAFETY, CORRECTIONS, AND SECURITY INDUSTRY PER 100 FULL-TIME WORKERS (2009)	
Occupation	Rate
Justice, public order, and safety activities (local government)	11.5
Public administration (local government)	7.9
Justice, public order, and safety activities (state government)	6.2
Public administration (state government)	4.3

Source: US Department of Labor

Job Benefits

Benefits aren't just extras. They not only make your life easier and safer, but they can also be worth 20 to 35 percent of your salary.

Standard job benefits usually include health insurance and paid holidays, sick time, and vacations. At most companies, new employees do not start receiving paid vacation time until they have been on the job for 90 days or more. The specific job benefits you receive will depend on several different factors. The size and type of organization you work for is one. How many years you have been on the job is another.

At some companies, job benefits have expanded in recent years to include more than health insurance, paid vacation, and holidays, and sick leave. Some expanded benefits may include

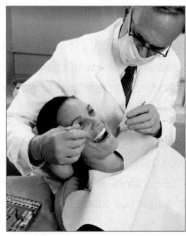

- dental, life, and disability insurance for the worker and his or her spouse or partner

- time off to care for sick children

- tuition assistance

- 401(k) plan, or a retirement plan in which employees invest a portion of their income, while employers match the contribution up to a specific amount

- child care assistance

In addition to these benefits, people in law enforcement often receive generous retirement benefits. Police officers may be able to take early retirement after 20 years of service, receiving half their salary in retirement. Full retirement benefits are often available after 30 years of service. Federal agents may qualify for special benefits and increased pay due to demanding work hours.

Labor Unions

A union is a group of workers who unite to bargain for job improvements.

Union leaders negotiate for better wages, increased benefits, better working conditions, and other job improvements. If an agreement is not reached, the union may use its most powerful tool—a strike. A strike occurs when employees stop working in an effort to force an employer to agree to the union's terms. In most cases, unions maintain strike funds, which provide partial salaries to striking workers.

When an agreement is reached between the union and company management, the company signs a labor contract. A labor contract is a legal agreement specifying wages, work hours, working conditions, and benefits. The union members must approve the contract before it goes into effect.

UNIONS IN LAW, PUBLIC SAFETY, CORRECTIONS, AND SECURITY

Less than 13 percent of all workers nationwide were union members in 2009. Workers in protective services, however, generally have a much higher union rate.

The International Association of Fire Fighters (IAFF) is the largest firefighters' labor organization in the country. With more than 298,000 members, the IAFF represents firefighters and emergency medical service providers. In addition, many states and even some cities have their own organizations for firefighters.

Most sworn police officers are members of the Fraternal Order of Police (FOP). This is the largest professional police organization in the United States. A variety of local unions for police officers exist all over the country.

Federal law enforcement officers may become members of the FOP. In addition, a number of associations exist for federal law enforcement officers, including the Federal Law Enforcement Officers Association and the FBI Agents Association. These organizations do not have collective bargaining powers. However, they do act as advocates for federal agents, providing publications, legal counsel, and a political voice in Washington for their members.

CHAPTER 6

INDUSTRY TRENDS

The law, public safety, corrections, and security industry is constantly changing. Technology has affected work processes and working conditions for jobs in this industry. In addition, new trends are affecting the practices and the workplace of many occupations.

Technology in the Law, Public Safety, Corrections, and Security Industry

It is hard to imagine how workers operated in the past without the benefit of today's technological advances. For example, law enforcement agencies could communicate with one another only by telephone or letter. Now they use the Internet and national crime databases. Police officers used to write all reports by hand. Now they complete and file reports using a computer. It is commonplace for officers to have laptop computers and Internet access in their patrol cars. Today computers and communication technology are vital to nearly all functions within this industry.

TECHNOLOGY IN LAW ENFORCEMENT SERVICES

Technological advances in law enforcement are helping officers identify, locate, and contain criminals. Criminal histories, penal codes, driving records, wanted suspect lists, and stolen property lists can be accessed easily. In addition, the ability of law enforcement agencies to share information securely can make solving crimes less problematic.

Biometric identification has grown in scope and accuracy over the years. Biometric identification includes any method of identification that uses unique biological features to confirm a person's identity. For example, face-recognition technologies can be used to compare the faces of criminals caught on video surveillance systems to mug shots in a police department's database.

Smartphone technology is making law enforcement more effective. For example, some cities use smartphone applications (apps) to allow citizens to report crimes. Tips can be sent quickly and easily to police departments. Language translation applications help officers communicate with a variety of people.

Advances in computer technology have allowed new analytical methods to develop. Crime mapping is the creation of detailed maps of where and when specific crimes have occurred. The maps can then be analyzed and used to track patterns of crime. In addition, analysis of evidence, including DNA analysis, has become more reliable as better technology has become available.

TECHNOLOGY IN LEGAL SERVICES

Improvements in communications systems has also helped the legal system. Real-time deposition technology allows lawyers to see depositions over the Internet. As the court reporter types the transcript, his or her computer automatically translates the shorthand notes into standard English. Transcribing depositions used to take several days. Now it is done instantly. This allows paralegals to prepare summaries, medical experts to prepare testimony, and lawyers to make notes, all at the same time.

Online law libraries minimize research time. Work that used to require a trip to the library can now be done by computer. Searchable online databases include legal documents and other resources.

TECHNOLOGY IN CORRECTION SERVICES

The use of technology to support traditional correctional strategies is known as technocorrections. Technocorrections meets the public's demand for tough sentences and greater control over offenders. At the same time, it reduces the population of overcrowded prisons.

Electronic monitoring of offenders has been used for many years. But new technologies can make these devices much more effective. GPS technology enables law enforcement officers to track and record an offender's movements. In general, those convicted of nonviolent crimes may be able to serve all or part of their sentences under house arrest. If an offender leaves his or her home or other approved location, an alarm goes off.

Biometric identification technology is being used to improve security in prisons. Fingerprint-recognition systems are used to allow access into and out of secure areas. Cards or passcodes, which can be lost or stolen, could be replaced with biometric scans. Visitors and guards could move about freely. Inmates would have fewer opportunities for escape.

TECHNOLOGY IN EMERGENCY AND FIRE MANAGEMENT SERVICES

Firefighting techniques such as fire modeling are more accurate due to advances in computer software. Fire modeling is the process of predicting the effects and behaviors of a fire. Computer programs analyze a building's layout, ventilation, and other factors to predict how and where flames will spread. These programs can predict how much heat and smoke may be produced by the fire and whether toxic gases may be present. This information can be used to fight fires.

Advanced fire safety technology allows firefighters to stay safe while fighting fires. One example is the Personal Alert Safety System (PASS). The first PASS devices contained sensors that monitored a firefighter's motion. If the firefighter stopped moving, the device would signal for help. New technologies are being developed to improve these devices. For example, heat sensors can warn a firefighter when conditions become extreme. GPS technology in the PASS devices can be used to locate a firefighter in a burning building.

Firefighters, EMTs, and paramedics have access to smartphone apps that help them act decisively in a crisis. One app makes the *Emergency Response Guidebook* available on a smartphone. This guidebook helps emergency responders when there is a crisis involving hazardous materials. Other apps help emergency responders record events, make calculations, and administer medical help.

TECHNOLOGY IN SECURITY AND PROTECTIVE SERVICES

Advances in security systems and the need for tighter information security have changed the security and protective services pathway. The security systems in buildings are becoming more sophisticated. Computer skills are becoming more and more vital to careers in this pathway.

Biometric identification is affecting the practices in this pathway. Facial-recognition technology can be used in areas where tight security is needed. Facial scans of travelers in an airport, for example, can be compared to photo databases of known terrorists. Fingerprint scans, iris scans, and even scans of the vein patterns in a person's hand can be used to restrict access to offices and ATMs. These technologies can be used to protect sensitive computer systems from unauthorized access.

Trends in the Law, Public Safety, Corrections, and Security Industry

This industry has seen several new trends in recent years. One trend has been the increasing effort to find methods that save money and treat suspects and convicts humanely while still protecting the public. Another trend has been toward a more diverse workforce.

Less-than-Lethal Force Technologies that allow officers to use less-than-lethal force are becoming more common. These devices allow officers to take control of difficult situations with less risk of serious injury or death. One popular less-than-lethal weapon is a stun gun. This is a handheld remote stun system. It subdues subjects with a jolt of electricity. It is intended to cause no long-term injury, and it does not affect the heart or pacemakers. Various nonlethal firearms, such as guns that have rubber bullets and pepperball guns, are also being used.

Alternative Sentencing Alternative sentencing refers to sentencing options other than traditional jail or prison terms. Alternative punishments include house arrest and electronic monitoring. Work release, counseling programs, drug treatment, and community service may also be alternative sentencing options. One goal of these programs is to reduce the prison population. In addition, these programs help offenders become contributing members of society.

Employment Trends In the modern workplace, a growing number of people work on a temporary basis. Some companies need workers only during busy times of the year. Others hire workers for short-term projects. For example, law firms often use temporary workers to help with big cases. Many companies hire temporary workers to fill in when employees are on vacation. Security guards are often temporary workers, sometimes employed by a security-staffing firm to provide security for special events.

Workplace Diversity More women and minorities are entering careers in law, public safety, corrections, and security. Many agencies have taken a more aggressive approach to recruiting women and people of diverse ethnic backgrounds. Some state and local fire and police departments have created plans to address the training and recruitment of a more diverse workforce.

CAREER RESOURCES

GENERAL CAREER RESOURCES

Career Key
www.careerkey.org
A free online self-assessment that identifies students' Holland career choice personality type.

CTE–Career Technical Education
www.careertech.org/career-clusters/glance/at-a-glance.html
A site featuring definitions and models of career clusters, along with resources about programs of study and real-world examples.

Dictionary of Occupational Titles
www.occupationalinfo.org
A searchable database of job titles and descriptions.

Mapping Your Future
www.mappingyourfuture.org
Career and education planning information for students, from middle school to adult.

Mind Tools
www.mindtools.com
A resource for developing the essential skills and techniques that will help workers excel in any chosen profession.

O*NET
http://online.onetcenter.org
An online resource center that offers skills profiles, details about hundreds of individual occupations, and crosswalks to codes from the *Dictionary of Occupational Titles*.

Occupational Outlook Handbook
www.bls.gov/oco/
The full text of the *Occupational Outlook Handbook* online provides information on education needs, earnings, prospects, descriptions, and conditions of hundreds of jobs.

Salary.com
www.salary.com
A nationwide database of salary information for hundreds of careers.

LAW, PUBLIC SAFETY, CORRECTIONS, AND SECURITY RESOURCES

American Association for Paralegal Education
www.aafpe.org
A national organization offering information about paralegal training.

American Bar Association
www.abanet.org
A professional association providing law school accreditation and information for legal professionals.

Corrections.com
www.corrections.com
A weekly news source providing news and information for corrections professionals.

Department of Justice
www.usdoj.gov
The executive department that enforces the law.

The Federal Bar Association
www.fedbar.org
A professional organization for private and government lawyers and judges involved in federal practice.

Federal Bureau of Investigation
www.fbi.gov
The main investigative arm of the Department of Justice.

Fraternal Order of Police
www.grandlodgefop.org
The world's largest organization of sworn law enforcement officers.

National Fire Academy
www.usfa.fema.gov/nfa
An academy that helps fire and emergency services professionals to deal with fire and related emergencies.

National Academies of Emergency Dispatch
www.emergencydispatch.org
An organization that supports and certifies professional medical, fire, and police dispatchers.

Security Guard
www.security-guard.org
A website providing information about the training and certification of security guards.

PREPARE

This section of *Career Companion: Law, Public Safety, Corrections, & Security* provides practice of the skills you will need for any career in law, public safety, corrections, and security. It is divided into three workplace skill areas:

READING FOR INFORMATION

LOCATING INFORMATION

APPLIED MATHEMATICS

At the beginning of each section is a list of specific skills presented. Also included are examples of situations in which these skills are likely to be used.

After practicing these workplace skills, you will be able to answer the following questions:

- How can I identify the main idea of a workplace document?
- What do I need to look for when following step-by-step instructions?
- How can workplace graphics help me make decisions?
- What types of calculations do I need to know to do my job?
- How can I solve problems using math operations?

Working your way through each skill area will help you prepare for a job in law, public safety, corrections, and security.

SKILLS PRACTICE
READING FOR INFORMATION

Reading for information is a key skill in the law, public safety, corrections, and security industry. You may spend your days researching court cases or studying contracts or other legal documents. No matter what the job, at some point you will need to read text to gather information. Before applying for a job, you will need to read a job description and understand the duties involved. You may be required to read a job application and understand the information it asks you to provide. Once hired, you may need to read the employee handbook, which lists rules and regulations for your position.

To succeed at a job, you must be able to understand the purpose of texts you encounter and identify the most important ideas and details. You must also know how to respond to them.

In the following pages, you will encounter a variety of workplace documents to read and interpret. You will also use a wide range of reading skills.

When you read a question on the following pages, think about what is being asked and how you might find the answer. Read the text carefully, focusing on the information you are asked to find or the steps you are asked to take. After you have chosen an answer, look back to make sure you have answered the question being asked.

Learning these key reading skills will speed your path to advancement in the law, public safety, corrections, and security industry.

KEY SKILLS FOR CAREER SUCCESS

Here are the topics and skills covered in this section and some examples of how you might use them to read different types of materials.

TOPIC	SKILL
Read and Understand Information in Workplace Documents	1. Identify Main Idea and Details 2. Identify Details that Are Not Clearly Stated

Example: As a paralegal, you will need to read contracts, depositions, and reference works to understand a case.

Follow Instructions from Workplace Documents	3. Understand and Apply Basic and Multi-Step Instructions 4. Apply Instructions to Unique Situations

Example: As an emergency medical technician, you may need to follow a set of specific instructions in order to save a person's life.

Define and Use Words in the Workplace	5. Determine the Meaning of New Words 6. Understand Unique Words and Acronyms 7. Understand and Apply Technical Terms and Jargon

Example: As a lawyer, you will need to be able to understand the terminology used in legal documents.

Understand and Follow Policies and Procedures in Workplace Documents	8. Apply Workplace Policies and Procedures 9. Understand the Rationale Behind Workplace Policies

Example: As a corrections officer, you may need to read policies that involve the treatment of inmates or new security procedures.

IDENTIFY MAIN IDEA AND DETAILS

When reading documents, such as an article about trends in security system design, workers in the law, public safety, corrections, and security industry need to be able to identify the main idea. They must also find details supporting the main idea. The main idea tells what the document is about. Details provide more information that helps explain the main idea.

NOTE FROM THE SUPERVISOR

Hi Bill:

I'm sure you're busy, but I need you to do a few extra things on your shift tonight. Paul called in sick, so I wasn't able to take care of everything during the day. Since you will be transitioning to the day shift, it will be good for you to start learning how to do these things anyway.

First, I need you to reset the security system with the new codes. You can find the instructions for how to do this in top left-hand drawer of your desk. Be sure to reset the codes at the beginning of your shift, because the old codes expire at midnight.

Next, please order the tapes needed for the security cameras. First, check how many tapes we have on hand. We need a total of 28 tapes, so subtract the number we have from 28. Fill out the order form on the desk and fax the order to the number on the form.

I hope I'm not giving you too much to do. If you have an emergency, feel free to give me a call. Good luck!

1. As a mall security officer, you receive this note from your supervisor when you arrive for your shift. What is the main idea of the second paragraph?

   A. You need to do a few extra things on your shift.

   B. You need to reset the security system.

   C. You must reset the codes at the beginning of your shift.

   D. You can find the instructions in the top left-hand drawer.

   E. The old codes expire at midnight.

2. Which detail helps you understand how to order the security tapes?

   A. The instructions are in the top left-hand drawer.

   B. You will be picking up the tapes.

   C. You should fill out the order form on the desk.

   D. You can call in case of an emergency.

   E. Be sure to reset the security codes at the beginning of your shift.

E-MAIL TO ABA SECURITY STAFF

ABA Security will be upgrading software on all computers on Friday. Please ensure that you have backed up all data on Thursday before you leave for the day.

In addition, all staff must receive training on the new database. The current customer database will no longer be available beginning July 1, so please make sure you have signed up for one of the two training sessions offered next week.

3. You are a security system designer for ABA Security, a private security company. You receive this office-wide e-mail. What is the main idea of the e-mail?

   A. All staff members must prepare for a change in software.

   B. The company will use new software in order to track customer orders.

   C. All staff members must take classes in order to keep their jobs.

   D. Volunteers are needed to train staff on the new database.

   E. The current customer database will no longer be available as of July 1.

4. Which detail describes what staff members will experience at work starting July 1?

   A. The company will be upgrading software.

   B. The staff will be in class learning the new software.

   C. The current database will no longer be available.

   D. Staff have a choice to attend training or not.

   E. The software will be backed up frequently.

ANSWER KEY

Item 1:   **B** You need to reset the security system.

Item 2:   **C** You should fill out the order form on the desk.

Item 3:   **A** All staff members must prepare for a change in software.

Item 4:   **C** The current database will no longer be available.

IDENTIFY DETAILS THAT ARE NOT CLEARLY STATED

Read and Understand Information in Workplace Documents

Follow Instructions from Workplace Documents

Define and Use Words in the Workplace

Understand and Follow Policies and Procedures in Workplace Documents

The details in workplace documents are not always clearly stated. For example, a police detective may have to draw conclusions about an eyewitness's testimony from a written statement. It may sometimes be necessary to infer, or make a logical guess, when a detail is suggested rather than stated.

NOTICE

Please be aware that smoking is not permitted near the entrances to the building. Building security will enforce this policy without exception. Those wishing to smoke outdoors must stand a minimum of 50 feet from any entrance. Management expects the cooperation of employees in following this policy. Any witnessed violation of this policy should be reported.

To accommodate smokers, a designated smoking room has been created at the west end of the building. The door must be closed whenever the room is being used for smoking. Smokers should place cigarette butts and ashes in the ashtrays provided in the designated smoking areas. Please be courteous and empty the ashtrays when they are filled.

1. You work as a sales representative at a home security company. What detail explains what people should do when using the smoking room?

   A. They should only use the room if it is unoccupied.

   B. They should stand at the room's entrance.

   C. They should check on the status of the ashtrays before leaving.

   D. They should close the door when they are finished using the room.

   E. They should stand at least 50 feet from the door.

2. As you return to work from a lunch break, you pass by two employees smoking in the entryway of the building. What would your employer expect you to do?

   A. Inform building security.

   B. Return to your desk.

   C. Speak to the smokers.

   D. Call human resources.

   E. Point out an ashtray.

BAILING SOMEONE OUT OF JAIL
WHAT HAPPENS IF THE DEFENDANT MISSES COURT?

The judge will issue a bench warrant for the defendant's arrest, and the bond will be in forfeit (default). In this instance, the only way you will get your cash bond back is for you to find the defendant and bring him or her back to jail within 90 days of the forfeiture OR for the defendant to be arrested by a law enforcement officer and brought back to jail within 90 days from the date the bond was forfeited.

If the defendant is returned to the jail by you or if the defendant is arrested before the 90 days have passed, then you will need to obtain the appropriate paperwork to request a refund from court personnel at your local courthouse. Complete the paperwork and file it with them to request that your money be mailed to you. If the defendant cannot be found within 90 days, you will lose the entire bond.

3. As a bail bondsperson, you give a pamphlet to each person who is interested in bailing out a person who has been arrested. A portion of the pamphlet is shown here. If a person pays a bond and the defendant does not make a scheduled court appearance, what can the payer do to get his or her money back?

   A. Appear in court and speak to the judge.

   B. Petition the court in writing.

   C. Wait 90 days before filing the necessary paperwork.

   D. Tell the bail bondsperson where the defendant is located.

   E. Return the defendant to jail yourself and complete the necessary paperwork.

4. What would happen if the defendant did not appear in court, but returned to jail the following week?

   A. The bond is forfeited and will not be returned.

   B. The bond is immediately refunded.

   C. The bond payer can request a refund.

   D. The bond payer must wait 90 days before acting.

   E. The bond payer must appear in court.

ANSWER KEY

Item 1:   **C** They should check on the status of the ashtrays before leaving.

Item 2:   **A** Inform building security.

Item 3:   **E** Return the defendant to jail yourself and complete the necessary paperwork.

Item 4:   **C** The bond payer can request a refund.

UNDERSTAND AND APPLY BASIC AND MULTI-STEP INSTRUCTIONS

It may be necessary to follow multi-step instructions in a variety of situations, such as when installing a new surveillance camera. Workers must read carefully to know when to take each step, and be able to apply the same instructions in a variety of situations.

INSTRUCTIONS FOR HANDLING NONCOMPLIANT BUSINESSES

The fire inspector or authorized agent must take the following steps if a business is found to be noncompliant with the fire safety code:

1. Identify and list the problems with the business and identify the relevant regulations in the fire safety code. Refer to the fire safety code document if you are unsure of the regulations.
2. Evaluate the hazards and determine what steps must be taken to bring the business into compliance with the safety code.
3. Provide the business with a written report listing the violations and remedies.
4. Set a date by which time the violations must be remedied.

1. In your work as a fire inspector, you must follow the procedures manual for inspecting businesses for fire safety violations. According to this section of the procedures manual, what must happen immediately after evaluating the hazards?

   A. Provide the business with a written report.

   B. Check that the violations have been remedied.

   C. Set a date to check the violations again.

   D. Determine the steps to be taken to bring the business into compliance.

   E. Identify and list the problems.

2. According to the document, when should the fire safety inspector consult the fire safety code document?

   A. when setting a date by which time the violations must be remedied

   B. when the inspector is determining which steps must be taken

   C. when the inspector is unsure of the regulations

   D. when producing a written report

   E. when selecting businesses to be inspected

A. AUTHORIZED VISITS

Each inmate is authorized two visits weekly. Visits from attorneys, clergy, and other "official" visitors are not counted against this quota. Official visitors are any government or social service agency personnel within the scope of their official duties. During an individual's reception period, while in quarantine status, visits will not be allowed except for bona fide family emergencies approved in advance by the Warden.

B. AUTHORIZED VISITORS

DOC staff must approve all visitors. Inmates will be authorized an unlimited number of family members on their visiting list. Non-family members will be limited in accordance with COR 305.02. All potential visitors will undergo a criminal records check. Inmates must provide a criminal records release authorization form (attachment 4) to all potential visitors 17 years of age or older. A visitor will not be added to an inmate's approved visiting list until the criminal release authorization form has been completed, notarized and a background check has been conducted. The inmate should attach the completed criminal record release authorization form to the inmate visitor request slip.

1. Visitors being taken off an inmate's list will be removed immediately and cannot be added to any inmate's visiting list for a one-year period.

3. As a correctional officer at a state prison, you are responsible for enforcing the visitor policy for inmates. An inmate has had two visitors this week. Which of the following visitors may be approved to visit today?

   A. the inmate's mother

   B. a friend who has been given a background check

   C. an attorney

   D. one of the people who has already visited this week

   E. a child of the inmate

4. Last month, an inmate had a dispute with a guest, and as a result the guest was taken off the inmate's approved visitor list. What must happen for the visitor to be added back to the approved visitor list?

   A. The inmate must request that the guest be added back to the list.

   B. The guest may not be added until a year has passed.

   C. The guest must pass a background check.

   D. The guest must be approved by DOC staff.

   E. A criminal release authorization form must be completed.

ANSWER KEY

Item 1:   **D** Determine the steps to be taken to bring the business into compliance.

Item 2:   **C** when the inspector is unsure of the regulations

Item 3:   **C** an attorney

Item 4:   **B** The guest may not be added until a year has passed.

SKILL

4

Read and
Understand
Information
in Workplace
Documents

**Follow
Instructions
from
Workplace
Documents**

Define and Use
Words in the
Workplace

Understand
and Follow
Policies and
Procedures
in Workplace
Documents

APPLY INSTRUCTIONS TO UNIQUE SITUATIONS

A set of instructions may call for different actions in different situations. For example, a fire inspector may follow a procedure manual to inspect different kinds of buildings, including homes, schools, and restaurants. The fire inspector needs to be able to apply the general inspection procedure to the inspection of all types of buildings.

NEW INTAKE FORMS

New intake forms have been created to replace the old universal forms. Please ensure you are using the appropriate form going forward. The new forms are tailored to different subjects using color coding.

The orange form is for juveniles who are interviewed as suspects in a crime. The green form is for juveniles who are witnesses or victims of crimes. Both new forms include information for parents or legal guardians because minors are entitled to have a parent or guardian present during any questioning. Information forms for adults are still printed on yellow paper. Please ensure that you are using the appropriate form moving forward.

1. While you are on duty as a police officer, a 16-year-old male comes to the police station because he was a witness to a robbery. What color form do you fill out?

    A. yellow

    B. green

    C. orange

    D. green and orange

    E. yellow and orange

2. When would you use an orange form?

    A. when an adult is a witness to a crime

    B. when an adult is a suspect in a crime

    C. when a juvenile is a witness to a crime

    D. when a juvenile is a victim of a crime

    E. when a juvenile is a suspect in a crime

HOW TO RESCUE SOMEONE WHO IS DROWNING

The most critical aspect of a lifeguard's job is to rescue a swimmer who is drowning. Follow these steps to give yourself the best chance of rescuing the victim:

1. The first step is to correctly identify a drowning victim. A drowning person may be thrashing his or her arms or may be nearly submerged, with just the mouth above water.

2. If you can do so without delay, alert other lifeguards or bystanders of the situation in case you need assistance.

3. Bring a rescue tube with you and approach the victim from behind. This will make it harder for the victim to push you underwater.

4. Place your arms under the victim's armpits and bend your arms up and back. Keep your rescue tube between yourself and the victim.

5. Calmly and gently pull the victim toward the shore. Once you have reached the shore, seek medical assistance.

3. As a lifeguard, you read these instructions to help you know how to rescue a swimmer who is drowning. One day you see a man drowning, and the only people nearby are other swimmers. What should you do?

   A. Swim out to save the victim without alerting anyone.

   B. Go looking for another lifeguard to tell him or her the situation.

   C. Announce the situation to the people nearby as you go in to help the victim.

   D. Ask one of the nearby swimmers to help you save the victim.

   E. Wait for another lifeguard to arrive before assisting the victim.

4. When you approach the drowning victim, you are facing him. What should you do?

   A. Go around the victim and approach him from behind.

   B. Approach the victim from the front to avoid wasting time.

   C. Grab the victim's hands to prevent him from pushing you down.

   D. Hand the victim the rescue tube.

   E. Ask the victim to turn his back to you.

ANSWER KEY

Item 1:   **B** green
Item 2:   **E** when a juvenile is a suspect in a crime
Item 3:   **C** Announce the situation to the people nearby as you go in to help the victim.
Item 4:   **A** Go around the victim and approach him from behind.

SKILL

5

Read and
Understand
Information
in Workplace
Documents

Follow
Instructions
from Workplace
Documents

**Define and
Use Words in
the Workplace**

Understand
and Follow
Policies and
Procedures
in Workplace
Documents

DETERMINE THE MEANING OF NEW WORDS

Law, public safety, corrections, and security workers occasionally come across words whose meaning is unclear or unfamiliar. For example, a traffic enforcement officer might encounter terms in a city road construction proposal that are not commonly used. Some words may be defined in the text, while others require the reader to determine the meaning. The text surrounding the word and the reader's background knowledge can help clarify the word's meaning.

LA PLAYA DEPARTMENT OF TRANSPORTATION

Repeat parking violators will be subject to special enforcement actions by the La Playa Department of Transportation, based on the state vehicle code, city municipal code, and DOT policy. An immobilizing device, called a "boot," will be placed by officers on vehicles with five or more outstanding parking citations. The boot also functions as a visual reminder to other drivers to comply with parking rules and pay outstanding citations.

Violators of parking laws in certain areas of the city will be subject to more severe violation penalties which will be issued by city traffic officers. Violators parked in tow and no-stopping zones will be issued a citation. The vehicle will also be immediately towed.

Teams of special enforcement officers from the La Playa Department of Transportation will be deployed in several high-traffic areas during rush hours to deter parking violations. These officers will patrol these areas to cite and ticket vehicles that park in "no stopping" lanes and impede traffic flow. Accidents are often the result of vehicles blocking lanes of traffic.

After the issuance of citations, the parking violations bureau is responsible for the collection of fees.

1. You are a traffic officer at the La Playa Department of Transportation. You see this document on the department's website. What is the meaning of the word **cite**?

    A. see

    B. ticket

    C. lead

    D. issue

    E. deploy

2. Based on the second to last paragraph of the document, what is one way to **impede** something?

    A. to carry it

    B. to lead it

    C. to issue it

    D. to send it

    E. to block it

WARDEN'S REPORT

Following a complaint by residents in the area on the night of Oct. 28, county game wardens responded to the area of County Road 37. They found two men loading the carcass of a freshly-killed deer into the back of a red pick-up truck. The subjects admitted to having killed the deer and their firearms were visible. Neither of the subjects possessed a license for hunting in the area. The wardens seized the deer and placed the subjects under arrest for unlawfully hunting without a license.

3. In your position as a document analyst in the county game warden's office, you are responsible for reviewing the warden's reports. In this report, what is the meaning of the word **seized**?

A. to make something unusable

B. to take possession of

C. to take into custody

D. to shake uncontrollably

E. to take photographs of

4. What are the **subjects** that are referenced in this report?

A. topics of a conversation

B. persons or things represented in a work of art

C. persons who live in a certain country

D. courses of study

E. people under the control of an authority

ANSWER KEY

Item 1:   **B** ticket

Item 2:   **E** to block it

Item 3:   **B** to take possession of

Item 4:   **E** people under the control of an authority

UNDERSTAND UNIQUE WORDS AND ACRONYMS

Read and
Understand
Information
in Workplace
Documents

Follow
Instructions
from Workplace
Documents

**Define and
Use Words in
the Workplace**

Understand
and Follow
Policies and
Procedures
in Workplace
Documents

Acronyms (words made from the initials of several words) and abbreviations may sometimes be used without explanation in work situations. For example, a forensic science technician might have instructions to access the IAFIS (Integrated Automated Fingerprint Identification System). To understand these terms, readers should use prior knowledge or study the surrounding text to determine their meaning.

CHANGES TO THE CRIME VICTIMS COMPENSATION FUND

The City of Springfield has recently reviewed its Crime Victims Compensation fund (CVC) and begun implementing changes to make sure that the city policy reflects the recommendations made by the US Department of Justice (DOJ). The changes to the CVC include a streamlined process for submitting claims and a dedicated office for coordinating benefits with insurance providers. The DOJ has provided detailed directions for how to set up protected CVC accounts in order to limit contact between criminals and their victims. Please review these instructions and implement protected CVC accounts for all new users of the CVC fund.

1. You work in Springfield as a crime victim advocate. The notice explains a change to the CVC program. What would you expect to find in the CVC?

    A. money to defend accused criminals

    B. money to pay victims of crimes for their losses

    C. files that describe what crimes were committed

    D. the city's policy on how to compensate crime victims

    E. bills from the US Department of Justice

2. You receive a file this week marked "DOJ." What does DOJ stand for?

    A. District of Jurisprudence

    B. Department of Jailers

    C. Deputy of Jury Trials

    D. Delay of Job Duties

    E. Department of Justice

TEACHERS WANTED

The State Department of Corrections is seeking Correctional Education Program Teachers to provide instruction in academic subjects to inmates who have not earned a high school diploma. Duties will include instructing inmates in core content areas at levels ranging from eighth to twelfth grade. Teachers are also responsible for developing lesson plans that incorporate recommendations from special education experts. As students may take state and national assessments, teachers are also expected to secure all testing instruments. Teachers will provide monthly work evaluations to management; attend training and meetings, and perform other duties appropriate to the assignment. Qualified candidates must have teaching certificates or at least two years' relevant teaching experience.

3. As a juvenile corrections officer you place an ad for teachers for the facility. What is the meaning of the word **core** as it is used in the second sentence?

    A. innermost

    B. largest

    C. central

    D. located in the middle

    E. additional

4. In the fourth sentence, what is an **instrument**?

    A. a person

    B. a musical object

    C. an instruction

    D. a tool

    E. a diploma

ANSWER KEY

Item 1:   **B** money to pay victims of crimes for their losses

Item 2:   **E** Department of Justice

Item 3:   **C** central

Item 4:   **D** a tool

UNDERSTAND AND APPLY TECHNICAL TERMS AND JARGON

Workers in law, public safety, corrections, and security need to understand workplace documents that use technical terms and jargon, or industry-specific language. Paralegals, for example, need to understand the terms used in legal documents, such as contracts and wills. They must be able to interpret the meanings of these terms and apply them to the situation at hand.

HARRIS COUNTY PAROLE SYSTEM
PRESS RELEASE

The number of parolees who have absconded parole supervision in Harris County has declined 13% from 2010. The absconders have failed to report to their parole appointments or check in with their parole officers. The location of more than 1,000 parole violators in 13 months is the fastest drop in the number of parolees-at-large in county history.

Harris County continues to reduce the number of parolees who may not have absconded, but who are noncompliant in other ways. Parole officers have a new way to report noncompliance, or not following the terms of parole. Instances of noncompliance include failure to complete random drug screens, report change of address or employment, or attend anger-management classes.

1. As a press agent for the Harris County Parole System, you send out this press release to local media. If someone is an **absconder**, what has he or she done?

    A. committed more than one crime

    B. avoided his or her duty as a parole officer

    C. failed to report to a parole officer

    D. failed to complete a drug test

    E. failed to attend anger-management classes

2. Which of the following is a sign that a parolee is **noncompliant**?

    A. being uncooperative or rude

    B. committing a crime

    C. agreeing to take a drug test

    D. denying that a crime has occurred

    E. breaking parole rules

JURY DUTY GUIDE

To be eligible to serve on a jury, you must be 18 years of age, a U.S. citizen, and a resident of the county for which you have been called. You are considered ineligible for the following reasons:

- You are a convicted felon or are under indictment.
- You or someone in your family works for the legislative branch of the local or state government.
- You do not speak, read, or write English.

WHAT HAPPENS NEXT?

If you are found to be eligible, you will be called to the courtroom where the judge will describe the case and introduce the lawyers. You will take an oath and undergo a process called voir dire, in which you will be asked about any knowledge you have and your feelings about the case. If selected, you will be given instructions on when to report for the trial.

AM I ALLOWED TO GO HOME EACH NIGHT?

Typically, jurors are allowed to go home at night. However, in rare cases, a judge may order that a jury be "sequestered" during the trial or while the jury is deliberating. A jury may be sequestered to reduce outside influences. While sequestered, transportation and lodging are provided.

3. As a lawyer, how would you explain **voir dire** to potential jurors?

   A. The lawyers make sure all potential jurors are present.

   B. Potential jurors tell whether they can serve on the jury or not.

   C. The judge asks the jurors to leave the courtroom.

   D. The members of the jury pool promise to be fair.

   E. Potential jurors are interviewed to ensure their impartiality.

4. What is the purpose of a jury being **sequestered**?

   A. to remove jurors who may already know about the case

   B. to allow the judge and lawyers to speak without the jury hearing

   C. to prevent jurors from hearing or seeing outside information about the trial

   D. to keep the jurors close to the court so the trial takes less time

   E. to give the lawyers a chance to see how the jurors behave

ANSWER KEY

Item 1:   **C** failed to report to a parole officer

Item 2:   **E** breaking parole rules

Item 3:   **E** Potential jurors are interviewed to ensure their impartiality.

Item 4:   **C** to prevent jurors from hearing or seeing outside information about the trial

APPLY WORKPLACE POLICIES AND PROCEDURES

Read and
Understand
Information
in Workplace
Documents

Follow
Instructions
from Workplace
Documents

Define and Use
Words in the
Workplace

**Understand
and Follow
Policies and
Procedures
in Workplace
Documents**

Most law, public safety, corrections, and security workers receive a policies and procedures manual when they begin work. It is important not just to understand the text of the manual, but to also apply the policies to their actual work situation. For example, correctional officers need to apply the rules for admitting visitors to specified visiting areas in a prison.

CODE OF CONDUCT

Liaisons in the drug and alcohol avoidance program must follow the program's spirit and philosophy. They must support the police department and the school they are affiliated with. Infractions against program policy will be handled strictly. Policy violations may result in decertification and loss of program affiliation.

1. Liaisons must not have engaged in any criminal misconduct.
2. Liaisons must always follow established policies and procedures.
3. Liaisons are forbidden from using the program name or logo in an unauthorized way.
4. Liaisons must behave professionally both at and outside of work.

1. As a law enforcement liaison, you are required to follow official rules. Why can you not use the program's name in an unauthorized way?

   A. Some uses of the name or logo might hurt the image or message of the program.

   B. Someone might use the wrong design for the logo.

   C. The program creators are concerned about copyrights.

   D. The program creators want total control over the program name.

   E. People who read the program name or logo without permission won't understand the program.

2. Why should liaisons' conduct outside of work always be professional?

   A. They are considered on duty at any time of day or night.

   B. As law enforcement, they should behave better than most people.

   C. They attend after-school activities with students.

   D. Professional behavior shows that liaisons believe what they teach.

   E. They follow the same standards schools have for teachers.

DISCLOSURE POLICY

The following guidelines should be strictly followed in any verbal or written communication, personal or professional, about the firm's work:

- Do not disclose the law firm's confidential information, such as current or past cases, clients, or terms of settlements, without permission. Ask permission to publish or report on meetings or conversations that occurred in the course of business within the firm.

- Do not reference the firm's staff, partners, or clients without permission.

- If you publish content that has something to do with your work at the firm, use a disclaimer such as: "These thoughts are my own and don't necessarily represent my employer's position or opinion." Seek permission before publishing any official firm business.

- Ensure that your conduct is consistent with the all policies listed in the Employee Handbook, Section 7.

3. As a paralegal, you receive a copy of your law firm's disclosure policy. What information can you share with your spouse?

  A. You can discuss anything as long as you use your personal e-mail.

  B. You can discuss the details of a case the lawyers are working on if you do not mention any names.

  C. You can say that a client won a case as long as you do not say how much money the client won.

  D. You can copy part of a company memo into an e-mail, but you cannot copy the entire memo.

  E. You can mention what you do at work as long as you do not include names or details.

4. In which situation would this policy also apply?

  A. posting a message on a blog about how a lawyer is handling a client's case

  B. responding to an invitation to an open house in your office building

  C. texting a reminder about ordering office supplies

  D. sending a request for a day off to your supervisor

  E. bookmarking the law firm's website in your Internet browser

ANSWER KEY

Item 1: **A** Some uses of the name or logo might hurt the image or message of the program.
Item 2: **D** Professional behavior shows that liaisons believe what they teach.
Item 3: **E** You can mention what you do at work as long as you do not include names or details.
Item 4: **A** posting a message on a blog about how a lawyer is handling a client's case

SKILL

9

Read and
Understand
Information
in Workplace
Documents

Follow
Instructions
from Workplace
Documents

Define and Use
Words in the
Workplace

**Understand
and Follow
Policies and
Procedures
in Workplace
Documents**

UNDERSTAND THE RATIONALE BEHIND WORKPLACE POLICIES

As with any industry, workplace policies in the law, public safety, corrections, and security industry are created for a reason. An OSHA inspector should understand the purpose behind safety codes. This knowledge helps staff to ensure the policies are being followed in the proper manner.

PERSONAL TIME POLICY

Dispatcher shifts are scheduled to ensure round-the-clock coverage. Unless a request for time off is caused by illness or a family emergency, dispatchers must give at least five days' notice for time off. Requests for vacation or personal days must be in writing and submitted to the Emergency Center manager. The manager will respond to requests as soon as possible. Note that if another dispatcher cannot be found to fill the shift, requests may be denied. Dispatchers should request assistance from coworkers to fill their shifts in case of emergencies.

1. You are a dispatcher in a 911 call center. This personal time policy is in your employee handbook. What is the rationale behind this policy?

   A. Employees should not take too much time off resulting in the manager having to pay overtime.

   B. Employees must give the manager enough time to find someone to work missed shifts.

   C. Employees should not go to work sick, spreading illness to coworkers.

   D. Managers work irregular shifts and need time to get requests.

   E. Managers need permission from dispatchers to change schedules.

2. Which of the following employees must make a request for time off at least five days in advance?

   A. an employee whose mother had a heart attack

   B. an employee who had a car accident

   C. an employee who has a daughter graduating college

   D. an employee whose child has chicken pox

   E. an employee who is a victim of a robbery

CRIMINAL HISTORY DISCLOSURE GUIDELINES

As a minor who has committed a crime, you may be able to receive deferred adjudication. If you accept and carry out the punishment the court directed, then the crime does not go on your legal record. If you successfully complete your sentence and the court dismisses the criminal charge(s), there are two issues of which you need to be aware.

Your arrest record and the record of the court's decision will be on record at the courthouse. The only way to make them private is to petition the court for an order of nondisclosure. This is only available for some Class C misdemeanors, and some Class C misdemeanors do not allow the order of nondisclosure until five years has passed.

Even though no conviction appears on your record with deferred adjudication, you may still have to disclose any convictions against you in certain circumstances. Many job applications ask you to list any convictions or guilty pleas to anything other than a minor traffic violation. In these instances, you must share your criminal history.

Please request a consultation with a clerk in our office if you have any questions about disclosure.

3. As a judge, you make decisions about people who receive deferred adjudication. A woman requests an order of nondisclosure. She was charged with a Class B misdemeanor. Which result is most likely?

    A. The deferred adjudication will be revoked by the court.

    B. The woman cannot get an order of nondisclosure.

    C. The woman will automatically get the order of nondisclosure.

    D. The record will not made private for five years.

    E. The woman will have to complete the punishment first.

4. A man who committed a robbery at age 15 contacts you. He pled guilty, served a sentence, and received an order of nondisclosure at 18. A new employer asked if he ever pled guilty to a crime. What should he do?

    A. Send his employer the order of nondisclosure.

    B. Tell his employer that he has not pled guilty to a crime.

    C. Tell his employer that he pled guilty to the robbery.

    D. Not agree to answer the employer's question.

    E. Tell the employer that he has not committed a crime as an adult.

ANSWER KEY

Item 1:   **B** Employees must give the manager enough time to find someone to work missed shifts.

Item 2:   **C** an employee who has a daughter graduating college

Item 3:   **B** The woman cannot get an order of nondisclosure.

Item 4:   **C** Tell his employer that he pled guilty to the robbery.

SKILLS PRACTICE

LOCATING INFORMATION

To succeed in a law, public safety, corrections, and security career, you must be able to effectively locate information. Information is presented in a variety of forms, including tables, graphs, maps, and diagrams. You may need to locate this information in graphics on a computer screen, in a document, or even posted on a bulletin board or wall.

Locating information means more than just finding it. It also means understanding it and making use of it in the job you do each day. It may also mean finding missing information and adding it to a document.

In the following pages, you will encounter a variety of workplace documents. You will be asked to find important information in these graphics. In some cases you must interpret information in these graphics. For example, you may need to compare data, summarize it, or sort through distracting information.

When you read a question on the following pages, think about what is being asked and how you might find the answer. Look at the graphic carefully, focusing on the information you are asked to find or the steps you are asked to take. After you have chosen an answer, look back to make sure you have answered the question being asked.

Learning these key locating information skills will speed your path to advancement in the law, public safety, corrections, and security industry.

KEY SKILLS FOR CAREER SUCCESS

Here are the topics and skills covered in this section and some examples of how you might use them to locate information in different types of graphics.

TOPIC	SKILL
Locate and Compare Information in Graphics	1. Find Information in Workplace Graphics 2. Enter Information into Workplace Graphics

Example: As a forensic science technician, you may need to examine photographs of crime scenes, fingerprints, and other visual evidence to help solve crimes.

Analyze Trends in Workplace Graphics	3. Identify Trends in Workplace Graphics 4. Compare Trends in Workplace Graphics

Example: As an emergency management specialist, you may need to use graphs and charts stay up-to-date on trends about natural disasters in your area.

Use Information from Workplace Graphics	5. Summarize Information in Workplace Graphics 6. Make Decisions Based on Workplace Graphics

Example: As a firefighter, you may need to use a map or diagram to find the best route through a burning building.

SKILL

1

Locate and
Compare
Information
in Graphics

Analyze Trends
in Workplace
Graphics

Use Information
from Workplace
Graphics

FIND INFORMATION IN WORKPLACE GRAPHICS

When reading workplace graphics, such as the floor plan of a building, law, public safety, corrections, and security workers must know what information to look for. The key information may be in one or more graphics. Workers must be able to sift through unimportant or distracting information to find what is needed.

Annual 9-1-1 Call Volume Report— Quarter One Results

911 Calls	Jan	Feb	Mar	1st Qtr
1995	12,300	13,685	12,520	38,505
1996	13,396	14,748	14,535	42,679
1997	11,697	12,630	13,985	38,312
1998	14,361	13,310	15,822	43,493
1999	15,904	14,820	17,649	48,373
2000	18,497	17,192	20,548	56,237
2001	21,091	19,198	20,974	61,263
2002	16,538	16,139	16,825	49,502
2003	17,366	16,954	23,323	57,643
2004	19,248	19,178	19,140	57,566
2005	18,907	17,413	14,395	50,715
2006	19,513	13,752	16,483	49,748
2007	19,360	18,044	21,221	58,625
2008	19,658	18,945	21,216	59,819
2009	19,844	18,331	21,712	59,887
2010	20,941	18,594	22,258	61,793
2011	20,351	19,751	22,812	62,914

1. You work as a paralegal, and your supervisor has asked you to analyze information on local 911 calls for an upcoming case. Which of the following years had the highest 911 call volume in the month of February?

A. 2011

B. 2001

C. 2003

D. 2004

E. 2005

2. Of the following choices, which year had over 60,000 emergency calls in the first quarter?

A. 2006

B. 2007

C. 2008

D. 2009

E. 2010

Accident Summary

Accident Type:	Electrocution
Weather Conditions:	Sunny, Clear
Type of Operation:	Steel Erection
Size of Work Crew:	3
Collective Bargaining	No
Competent Safety Monitor on Site:	Yes - Victim
Safety and Health Program in Effect:	No
Was the Worksite Inspected Regularly:	Yes
Training and Education Provided:	No
Employee Job Title:	Steel Erector Foreman
Age & Sex:	43-Male
Experience at this Type of Work:	4 months
Time on Project:	4 Hours

3. You are an accident investigator filling out a report about a recent accident. Based on the accident summary, what happened?

   A. A worker was electrocuted at a steel erection site.

   B. An electrical wire fell, causing an electrical outage.

   C. Bad weather conditions caused an electrocution.

   D. A worker hit an electric fence, causing an electrical outage.

   E. Due to the lack of inspection, electrical wires were damaged.

4. Was there a safety monitor on the site of the incident?

   A. no

   B. yes, the site chief

   C. yes, the victim

   D. yes, a union representative

   E. yes, a company trainer

ANSWER KEY

Item 1: **A** 2011

Item 2: **E** 2010

Item 3: **A** A worker was electrocuted at a steel erection site.

Item 4: **C** yes, the victim

ENTER INFORMATION INTO WORKPLACE GRAPHICS

It may be necessary at times to add information to graphics as part of a job in the law, public safety, corrections, and security industry. A paramedic may need to complete a chart indicating a patient's vital statistics and any medical treatment the patient received on the way to the hospital. Knowing how to correctly add information to graphics is an important skill in this industry.

AFFIDAVIT OF MALE APPLICANT FOR MARRIAGE LICENSE

Age _27_   Birthdate _2/18/1983_ Birthplace _Seattle, Washington_   Phone Number _111-555-0999_

Single ☐   Widowed ☐   Divorced ☐   Under Control of Guardian ☐

Address _134 S. Wentwood Drive, Apartment 3B, Seattle, WA, 12345_

Address _N/A_
        (past six months)

I, the undersigned, do solemnly swear or affirm that the information on this form is true and correct. I am eighteen (18) years of age or older, or qualify as designated through the consent of a parent or guardian. I am not afflicted with any contagious sexually transmitted diseases, or if present, the condition is known to the female applicant. I am not nearer of kin to the female applicant than second cousin. **Marriage license is not valid for 3 days from date of application and shall become void if marriage is not solemnized within sixty (60) days of issuance of the license.**

☑ He is at least 17 years of age and his parent's or guardian's written consent, in accordance with the law, accompanies this application.

NAME _Adam King_   **SIGNATURE** _Adam King_

Subscribed and sworn to before me this _5_ day of _January_, 20_11_.

JANE M. SMITH, SMITH COUNTY AUDITOR by:_____
                                            Notary or Deputy Auditor

---

1. You are a court clerk processing an application for a marriage license. What information does the applicant still need to fill in?

   A. address

   B. signature

   C. age

   D. birthdate

   E. marital status

2. Where would a notary place his or her official stamp or signature on the completed form?

   A. NAME line

   B. BIRTHPLACE line

   C. PHONE NUMBER line

   D. NOTARY OR DEPUTY AUDITOR line

   E. ADDRESS line

Ambulance Equipment Standards

Ambulances shall have as a minimum the following equipment. All equipment must be kept on board at all times.

☐ 24 disaster tags (met-tags or district approved equivalents)
☐ 1 sterile saline (500 cc. container, must not be past expiration date)
☐ EMS HEAR Radio (meeting the requirements of § 2.423)
☐ A portable suction unit with wide bore tubing and a pharyngeal suction tip.
☐ A fixed oxygen system with M-size tank or equivalent and a variable flow regulator.
☐ 2 D-sized portable oxygen tanks or equivalent
☐ Oxygen connector tubing, assorted adult and child size masks
☐ 1 adult bag valve mask unit capable of delivering greater than 90% oxygen, adult mask, and child mask.
☐ A pediatric bag mask unit with oxygen reservoir is optional.
☐ 2 adult, 2 child, 2 infant oral airways
☐ 1 traction splint
☐ 2 short spineboards of wood or metal with 2 straps each, 9' minimum length, KEDs, Kansas Boards or similar devices.
☐ 2 long spineboards of wood or metal with 3 straps each, 9' min. length.
☐ 2 long arm splints. Cardboard, wood, pneumatic, etc. are acceptable.
☐ 2 long leg splints. Cardboard, wood, pneumatic, etc. are acceptable.
☐ Cervical collars. At least 1 large, 2 medium, and 1 small
☐ An adequate supply of bandaging materials to include:
    large and small sterile dressings, 10" x 30" multi-trauma dressings or equivalent,
    roller bandage 3" or larger width, triangular bandages, adhesive tape - 1" or larger width rolls,
☐ 2 sterile burn sheets
☐ 1 obstetrical kit, prepackaged commercial unit or equivalent
☐ 1 Automated External Defibrillator (AED), or, for Paramedic licensed services, a manual defibrillator.
☐ 1 adult sphygmomanometer and stethoscope
☐ 1 pediatric sphygmomanometer
☐ 1 trauma shears
☐ 1 activated charcoal not past expiration date
☐ 2 flashlights (with 2 D size batteries or larger)
☐ 10 lb. ABC fire extinguisher or two 5 lb. units.
☐ 1 wheeled ambulance cot with sturdy vehicle fastening hardware, linen,
☐ pillows, blankets, and patient safety straps.

3. As an EMT, you are conducting an inventory of your ambulance's equipment. How many cervical collars should you have on board?

   A. 1

   B. 2

   C. 3

   D. 4

   E. 5

4. Which of the following pieces of equipment is optional?

   A. long arm splint

   B. trauma shears

   C. sterile burn sheets

   D. portable suction unit

   E. pediatric bag mask unit

ANSWER KEY

Item 1: **E** marital status
Item 2: **D** NOTARY OR DEPUTY AUDITOR line
Item 3: **D** 4
Item 4: **E** pediatric bag mask unit

SKILL

3

Locate and
Compare
Information
in Graphics

**Analyze
Trends in
Workplace
Graphics**

Use Information
from Workplace
Graphics

IDENTIFY TRENDS IN WORKPLACE GRAPHICS

Law, public safety, corrections, and security workers must sometimes analyze graphics to identify trends. They might search for data that has increased or decreased over time. An emergency planner, for example, might use a graph of temperature and precipitation trends to determine the risk of fires in an area. Being able to identify common trends from several pieces of data can be helpful in a variety of jobs in this industry.

One-Year Recidivism Rates

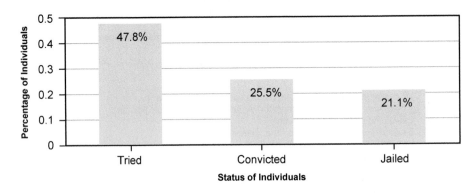

1. Recidivism is repeating a crime after having been convicted. You are a police chief studying a graph of recidivism rates in your city so that you can provide training for your officers. What trend do you notice?

   A. Individuals who were jailed have the highest recidivism rate.

   B. Individuals who were convicted have the highest recidivism rate.

   C. Individuals who were convicted have the lowest recidivism rate.

   D. Individuals who were tried have the lowest recidivism rate.

   E. Individuals who were tried have the highest recidivism rate.

2. The graph shows the percentage of individuals who were tried in court, convicted (found guilty) of an offense, and jailed. Based on the graph, what appears to be the best method for reducing recidivism?

   A. jailing

   B. convicting

   C. trying

   D. trying and convicting

   E. convicting, but not jailing

Authorized/Adopted Rules

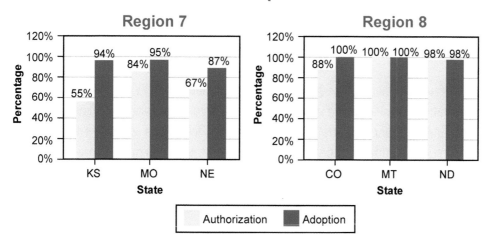

Region 7

Region 8

Authorization   Adoption

3. As an emergency management and coordinator you are reviewing state compliance with governmental regulations for the disposal of hazardous waste. Based on this data, what trend do you notice in region 7 about the relationship between authorization by government agencies and rule adoption by the state?

   A. All three states have adopted more rules than required.

   B. All three states have adopted fewer rules than required.

   C. MO has adopted all rules, while KS and NE have not.

   D. KS and NE have adopted all rules, while MO has not.

   E. KS is in violation of rule authorization.

4. Based on the graphs, how does region 8 compare with region 7?

   A. The trend is exactly the same.

   B. Unlike region 7, some region 8 states have more authorized than adopted rules.

   C. Unlike region 7, region 8 states have adopted more rules than were authorized.

   D. Unlike region 7, some region 8 states have the same number of authorized as adopted rules.

   E. None of the region 8 states have adopted all the authorized rules.

ANSWER KEY

Item 1: **E** Individuals who were tried have the highest recidivism rate.

Item 2: **A** jailing

Item 3: **A** All three states have adopted more rules than required.

Item 4: **D** Unlike region 7, some region 8 states have the same number of authorized as adopted rules.

Locate and
Compare
Information
in Graphics

**Analyze
Trends in
Workplace
Graphics**

Use Information
from Workplace
Graphics

COMPARE TRENDS IN WORKPLACE GRAPHICS

When reviewing workplace graphics, it may be necessary to compare information in one or more graphics. A police chief may need to review data about the frequency of different types of crimes in various areas of a city to determine the number of patrol officers per shift. Workers must know how different graphics relate to each other, and be able to compare information and trends within them.

Groups Adopting a VPP

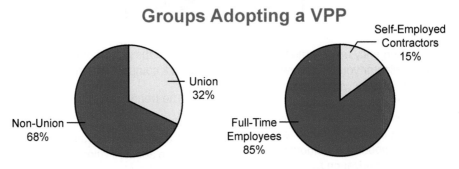

Union vs. Non-Union Employees   Full-Time vs. Contractors

1. In your job as a product safety consultant you are evaluating the percentages of worksites and employees who have adopted a Voluntary Protection Program (VPP). What subgroup has the highest percentage of program adoption?

    A. union

    B. non-union

    C. self-employed contractors

    D. full-time employees

    E. part-time employees

2. How does the percentage of self-employed contractors who adopted a Voluntary Protection Program compare to program adoption among union members?

    A. More than twice as many union members participated in a VPP than self-employed contractors.

    B. More than twice as many self-employed contractors participated in a VPP than union members.

    C. About the same percentage of union members participated in a VPP as self-employed contractors.

    D. More than three times as many union members participated in a VPP than self-employed contractors.

    E. More than three times as many self-employed contractors participated in a VPP than union members.

Statistics of Cold Hits and Success Rates Based on NDIS Data from CODIS

State	Number of *				
	*Offender Profiles	*Forensic samples	*CODIS Labs	*Investigations Aided	Success Rate (= No. of Cases Aided/No. of Forensic Samples)
Alabama	163,656	3,944	4	2,234	0.566430
Alaska	11,920	704	1	228	0.323864
Arizona	137,639	7,281	7	2,365	0.324818
Arkansas	92,366	2,303	1	505	0.219279
California	1,061,374	18,519	20	7,333	0.395972
Colorado	95,267	3,856	5	925	0.239886
Connecticut	43,397	2,403	1	845	0.351644
Delaware	3,557	275	1	10	0.036364
DC/FBI-Lab	63,924	1,757	4	274	0.155948
Florida	523,834	21,075	10	8,593	0.407734
Georgia	156,887	6,868	3	1,742	0.253640
Hawaii	11,527	177	1	42	0.237288

3. In your job as a forensic DNA analyst, you are preparing a report for your supervisor. The Combined DNA Index System, or CODIS, is a computer software program that operates databases of DNA profiles. What does this table tell you?

   A. A greater number of CODIS labs results in a greater success rate.

   B. A greater number of CODIS labs results in fewer investigations aided.

   C. A greater number of offender profiles results in a greater number of investigations aided.

   D. A greater number of forensic samples results in a lower success rate.

   E. A greater number of offender profiles results fewer CODIS labs.

4. Which of the following states had the highest success rate using information from CODIS?

   A. Alaska

   B. California

   C. Delaware

   D. Florida

   E. Alabama

ANSWER KEY

Item 1: **D** full-time employees

Item 2: **A** More than twice as many union members participated in a VPP than self-employed contractors.

Item 3: **C** A greater number of offender profiles results in a greater number of investigations aided.

Item 4: **E** Alabama

SUMMARIZE INFORMATION IN WORKPLACE GRAPHICS

When workers look at a graphic such as a diagram or a bar graph, they need to analyze and make sense of the information. It may be necessary to summarize the information, or boil it down to the most important facts. For example, a security management specialist might have to summarize the features shown on a security system diagram for a client. Being able to summarize allows workers to make sense of varying information.

2010 HazMat Summary By Hazardous Materials Class

Hazardous Materials Class	Injuries				
	Incidents	Hospitalized	Non-Hospitalized	Fatalities	Damages
Flammable-Combustible Liquid	7,117	8	35	3	$27,145,047
Corrosive Material	3,966	9	83	0	$16,929,146
Nonflammable Compressed Gas	590	1	12	2	$1,938,986
Oxidizer	423	0	0	0	$1,162,252
Poisonous Materials	265	0	15	0	$315,831
Flammable Solid	86	0	0	0	$10,800
Infectious Substance(Etiologic)	84	0	3	0	$0
Poisonous Gas	30	1	1	0	$365,989
Radioactive Material	20	0	0	0	$335,000
Spontaneously Combustible	10	0	0	0	$9,300
Explosive Mass Explosion Hazard	5	0	0	0	$38,000
Dangerous When Wet Material	5	0	0	0	$0
Explosive Fire Hazard	1	0	0	0	$900
Total – 2010	12,602	19	149	5	$48,251,251

1. As a hazardous materials specialist, you are reviewing information on hazardous material incidents in 2010. According to the chart, which of the following statements is true about the order of the entries?

   A. The table is organized by cost of damages.

   B. The table is organized by class of haz-mat incident.

   C. The table is organized by number of incidents.

   D. The table is organized by number of fatalities.

   E. The table is organized by injuries.

2. The table indicates that which of the following hazardous materials classes caused the most incidents in 2010?

   A. flammable-combustible liquids

   B. explosive fire hazards

   C. radioactive materials

   D. infectious substances

   E. poisonous materials

Global Trends in Terror Attack Methods and Victims

Deaths by Method

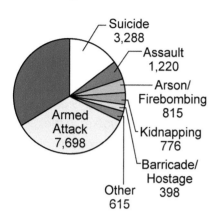

Suicide 3,288
Assault 1,220
Arson/ Firebombing 815
Kidnapping 776
Barricade/ Hostage 398
Other 615
Armed Attack 7,698

Deaths by Victim Category

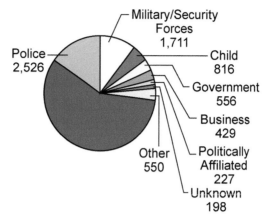

Military/Security Forces 1,711
Police 2,526
Child 816
Government 556
Business 429
Politically Affiliated 227
Unknown 198
Other 550

3. In your job as an intelligence operations specialist, one of your responsibilities is reviewing the latest report from the counterterrorism center. According to the graphs, which of the following would be the most likely homicide to occur?

   A. a police officer killed by arson

   B. a civilian killed after a kidnapping

   C. a government official killed in a hostage situation

   D. a police officer killed in an armed attack

   E. a civilian killed in an armed attack

4. What is the likely risk of being killed in hostage situation to a business person?

   A. very high risk

   B. high risk

   C. moderate risk

   D. low risk

   E. no risk

ANSWER KEY

Item 1:   **C** The table is organized by number of incidents.

Item 2:   **A** flammable-combustible liquids

Item 3:   **E** a civilian killed in an armed attack

Item 4:   **D** low risk

MAKE DECISIONS BASED ON WORKPLACE GRAPHICS

After analyzing the information in a workplace graphic, the next step is often to make a decision or take action as a result of the analysis. A worker in the law, public safety, corrections, and security industry might need to decide on the best path to a traffic accident or fire based on maps showing current road construction. Making the right decisions based on graphical information can help make workers more effective in their jobs.

Occupational Injuries, 2007-2008

Event/Exposure	2007	2008
Contact with electric current	212	192
Contact with overhead power lines	94	102
Contact with temperature extremes	40	35
Exposure to caustic, noxious, or allergenic substances	161	127
Inhalation of substance	64	56
Oxygen deficiency	82	77
Drowning, submersion	62	59
Fires and explosions	152	173

1. You are a paramedic interested in receiving additional training in treating workplace injuries. Based on this chart, which type of event might you consider focusing on because of the increased number of events over the past few years?

   A. contact with electric current

   B. contact with temperature extremes

   C. oxygen deficiency

   D. drowning, submersion

   E. fires and explosions

2. Which type of event might you focus on based on total number of events?

   A. contact with electric current

   B. contact with temperature extremes

   C. inhalation of substance

   D. oxygen deficiency

   E. drowning, submersion

The safest place in a vehicle for all children is the rear seat. Never place a rear-facing infant seat in the front seat of a vehicle with an activated passenger-side air bag.

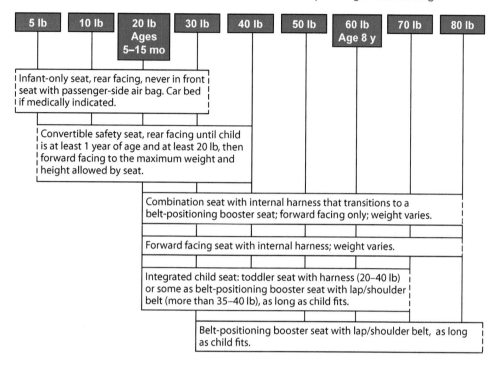

3. As a sheriffs' department officer, you conduct child safety seat workshops with the public. You are focusing today's workshop on choosing the right child safety seat. A parent has asked you what seat to choose for a newborn child. What do you recommend?

   A. infant-only seat, rear facing

   B. convertible safety seat, front facing

   C. combination seat with harness

   D. integrated child seat

   E. belt-positioning booster seat

4. A parent asks you if a 70-pound child still needs to use a child safety seat, even after the child is old enough by law to ride without a child seat. What do you tell the parent is the safest course of action?

   A. The child should ride with just the lap belt.

   B. The child should ride with just the lap belt, but only in the back seat.

   C. The child should ride in a convertible child safety seat.

   D. The child should ride in an infant-only seat, rear-facing.

   E. The child should ride in a belt-positioning booster seat.

ANSWER KEY

Item 1: **E** fires and explosions

Item 2: **A** contact with electric current

Item 3: **A** infant-only seat, rear facing

Item 4: **E** The child should ride in a belt-positioning booster seat.

SKILLS PRACTICE

APPLIED MATHEMATICS

Using applied mathematics will help you succeed in the law, public safety, corrections, and security career cluster. Some mathematical skills required for this cluster can be very complex, such as when a fire investigator identifies how a fire started based on calculations and observations. Other skills are very simple, such as calculating the number of cells available in a jail. Some key skills include multiplying and dividing, finding percentages, and adding fractions.

In the following pages, you will encounter a variety of applied math problems. Each item describes a real-life situation in a law, public safety, corrections, or security career. You will be asked to solve the problems by applying your mathematical skills. You may need to use arithmetic, geometry, or measurement skills, for example.

When you read a question on the following pages, think about what is being asked and how you might find the answer. Read the text carefully, focusing on the information you are asked to find or the steps you are asked to take. After you have chosen an answer, look back to make sure you have answered the question being asked.

By learning and practicing these key mathematical skills, you will put yourself in a better position to succeed in the law, public safety, corrections, and security industry.

KEY SKILLS FOR CAREER SUCCESS

Here are the topics and skills covered in this section and some examples of how you might use them to solve workplace problems.

TOPIC	SKILL
Perform Basic Arithmetic Calculations to Solve Workplace Problems	1. Solve Problems with Whole Numbers and Negative Numbers 2. Use Fractions, Decimals, and Percentages to Solve Workplace Problems

Example: As a mediator, you may need to work with percentages to help the different parties in a conflict agree on a financial settlement.

Apply Computations to Solve Workplace Problems	3. Use General Problem Solving 4. Solve Problems in Geometry

Example: As a forest firefighter, you may need to calculate the perimeter of a forest that is burning.

Solve Measurement Problems	5. Calculate with Conversions and Formulas 6. Manipulate Formulas to Solve Problems

Example: As a police officer working at the scene of an accident, you may need to use a formula to calculate the speed of a car based on the length of the skid marks.

Make Spending Decisions to Solve Workplace Problems	7. Calculate Costs and Discounts 8. Make Consumer Comparisons

Example: As a security management specialist, you may need to compare the value of different security system components in order to update a system.

SOLVE PROBLEMS WITH WHOLE NUMBERS AND NEGATIVE NUMBERS

Perform Basic Arithmetic Calculations to Solve Workplace Problems

Apply Computations to Solve Workplace Problems

Solve Measurement Problems

Make Spending Decisions to Solve Workplace Problems

Addition, subtraction, multiplication, and division of whole numbers are important skills in any career cluster, and law, public safety, corrections, and security is no exception. A lifeguard, for example, may need to add and subtract the number of swimmers entering and exiting a pool area to make sure the number does not exceed the maximum allowed.

1. You are an animal control officer working in a large city. You work four hours in the morning and four hours in the afternoon. In the morning, you pick up 11 stray dogs. In the afternoon, you pick up 6 stray dogs. How many dogs do you pick up?

   A. 8

   B. 9

   C. 14

   D. 17

   E. 20

2. You are a self-employed private investigator. The business you run has a total of four private investigators employed. There are 12 new cases, and you plan to assign an equal number of cases to each investigator. How many assignments does each investigator get?

   A. 2

   B. 3

   C. 4

   D. 8

   E. 15

3. You are a lifeguard working at a public beach. Today, you have been instructed to purchase sunscreen for the lifeguard staff. You purchase 11 boxes of sunscreen, and each box contains twelve 12-ounce bottles of sun screen. Your boss wants to know how many bottles of sunscreen were purchased so he can figure out how quickly the employees use sunscreen. How many bottles of sunscreen did you purchase?

   A. 111

   B. 131

   C. 132

   D. 141

   E. 147

4. In your work as a probation officer, you check in with paroled criminals and confirm that they are not violating their parole conditions. Yesterday you were supposed to hear from 13 parolees, but only 10 parolees contacted you. How many parolees still need to contact you?

   A. 3

   B. 5

   C. 7

   D. 11

   E. 13

5. As an emergency management coordinator in Wisconsin, one of your duties is to prepare for harsh winter weather. There was a blizzard yesterday, and temperatures sank to –12 degrees Fahrenheit. Today the temperature rose to 14 degrees Fahrenheit. How much warmer is it today than it was yesterday?

   A. 11° F

   B. 14° F

   C. 21° F

   D. 23° F

   E. 26° F

6. You are an emergency preparedness coordinator working for a city in Alaska. The city shuts down public schools whenever the temperature reaches –30 degrees Celsius. Today the temperature is –22 degrees Celsius. How much colder would it have to be for the schools to shut down?

   A. 5° C

   B. 8° C

   C. 14° C

   D. 20° C

   E. 21° C

7. You are an intelligence analyst. You have been given access to a budget of $1,500 to purchase image processing software. The best image processing software costs $1,799. What would the balance of the budget be if you purchased the best software?

   A. –$399

   B. –$349

   C. –$333

   D. –$299

   E. –$249

8. You are a loss prevention specialist. One of your duties is to analyze a company's records to determine if a company may go bankrupt in the near future and to help prevent bankruptcy. The company you are reviewing now currently has a net worth of $100,000. The model you have constructed predicts that the company will lose $140,000 over the next year. If the model is correct, what will the company's net worth be in a year?

   A. –$140,000

   B. –$100,000

   C. –$80,000

   D. –$40,000

   E. $40,000

ANSWER KEY

Item 1: **D** 11 + 6 = 17

Item 2: **B** 12 ÷ 4 = 3

Item 3: **C** 11 × 12 = 132

Item 4: **A** 13 – 10 = 3

Item 5: **E** 14 – (–12) = 26° F

Item 6: **B** –22 – (–30) = 8° C

Item 7: **D** 1,500 – 1,799 = –$299

Item 8: **D** 100,000 – 140,000 = –$40,000

USE FRACTIONS, DECIMALS, AND PERCENTAGES TO SOLVE WORKPLACE PROBLEMS

Law, public safety, corrections, and security workers come across quantities represented in many different ways. A forensic science technician may measure the volume and mass of chemicals and samples of evidence. The ability to perform workplace calculations using different forms is an important skill.

1. You are a state game warden working in New York. In New York, it is illegal to catch female crabs that are bearing eggs. Over the past month, 30 percent of the tickets you issued were for crabbers catching egg-bearing crabs. What fraction of tickets issued last month were for crabbers catching egg-bearing crabs?

   A. $\frac{1}{30}$

   B. $\frac{1}{10}$

   C. $\frac{3}{20}$

   D. $\frac{1}{5}$

   E. $\frac{3}{10}$

2. You are a law clerk working for a major law firm. The case you are working on has required several legal documents to be retrieved from storage. You have retrieved three fifths of the documents needed. What percentage of the documents have you retrieved?

   A. 60%

   B. 65%

   C. 69%

   D. 75%

   E. 76%

3. You are a corrections educator assisting inmates with their continuing education. In the facility you work at, $\frac{1}{3}$ of the inmates are working to get their high school diploma and $\frac{1}{4}$ of the inmates are working on college-level courses. What fraction of the inmates are working on educational programs with you?

   A. $\frac{7}{12}$

   B. $\frac{2}{3}$

   C. $\frac{3}{4}$

   D. $\frac{7}{8}$

   E. $\frac{11}{12}$

4. You are a fire code inspector. Of the properties you inspected today, 21 percent failed the inspection. Also, 32 percent of the properties had to have another inspection scheduled. The remaining properties passed inspection. What percentage of the properties did not pass inspection?

   A. 44%

   B. 50%

   C. 53%

   D. 57%

   E. 59%

5. You are an animal control officer. You need to store two animal cages in a warehouse. You want to stack the two dog cages but must first check to see that the shelves in the warehouse are tall enough. The first dog cage is $\frac{3}{2}$ foot tall and the second dog cage is $\frac{5}{4}$ foot tall. How tall must the shelves be?

   A. 2 foot

   B. $2\frac{3}{4}$ feet

   C. $2\frac{1}{2}$ feet

   D. 3 feet

   E. $3\frac{1}{4}$ feet

6. In your job as a magistrate working in a state court, your job is to hear and settle minor civil disputes. Last month, $\frac{1}{8}$ of your cases were settled outside of court and $\frac{3}{16}$ of your cases were reassigned to a judge. The rest of the cases were resolved in court. Your supervisor is considering hiring another magistrate to help with civil disputes and wants to know what fraction of your cases you are not responsible for resolving. What fraction of the cases you heard last month were not settled in your court?

   A. $\frac{1}{8}$

   B. $\frac{5}{16}$

   C. $\frac{1}{2}$

   D. $\frac{7}{8}$

   E. $\frac{15}{16}$

7. You are a state trooper. Today, you spent three hours patrolling highways. During each of these hours, you drove $10\frac{1}{2}$ miles. At the end of the day you fill out a gas reimbursement sheet which requires you to record the number of miles you drove during the day. How many miles did you drive while patrolling highways today?

   A. 25

   B. 27

   C. 28.5

   D. 30.5

   E. 31.5

8. You are a civil division deputy sheriff. Several members of your precinct have caught the flu, so you are required to work overtime. Your overtime salary is $20.70 an hour, and you work $5\frac{1}{2}$ hours overtime. How much do you earn for working overtime?

   A. $97.98

   B. $101.45

   C. $113.85

   D. $115.00

   E. $120.85

ANSWER KEY

Item 1: **E** 30% = 0.3 = $\frac{3}{10}$

Item 2: **A** $\frac{3}{5}$ = 0.6 = 60%

Item 3: **A** $\frac{1}{3} + \frac{1}{4} = \frac{4}{12} + \frac{3}{12} = \frac{7}{12}$

Item 4: **C** 21% + 32% = 53%

Item 5: **B** $\frac{3}{2} + \frac{5}{4} = \frac{6}{4} + \frac{5}{4} = \frac{11}{4} = 2\frac{3}{4}$ feet

Item 6: **B** $\frac{1}{8} + \frac{3}{16} = \frac{2}{16} + \frac{3}{16} = \frac{5}{16}$

Item 7: **E** $10\frac{1}{2} \times 3 = (10 + \frac{1}{2}) \times 3 = 30 + \frac{3}{2} = 31\frac{1}{2} = 31.5$

Item 8: **C** $5\frac{1}{2}$ = 5.5; 5.5 × 20.70 = $113.85

USE GENERAL PROBLEM SOLVING

Some mathematical calculations require more than one operation. Fire captains, for example, may need to inventory their equipment, decide what new equipment must be ordered, and calculate the total cost of the new equipment. Being able to quickly perform such calculations can improve a law, public safety, corrections, and security worker's efficiency.

1. You are a computer forensics examiner. Your job is to search confiscated computers for evidence of illegal activities. At the start of the week, your team had 23 computers to search. During the week, your lab received 15 more computers that needed to be searched and your team searched 21 computers. How many computers need to be searched at the end of the week?

   A. 2

   B. 15

   C. 17

   D. 21

   E. 23

2. You are a fire captain. You are ordering new fire extinguishers for the department. Each fire extinguisher costs $75 and contains 2.5 pounds of carbon dioxide. How much does it cost to purchase enough fire extinguishers to have 10 pounds of carbon dioxide?

   A. $75.00

   B. $150.00

   C. $187.50

   D. $300.00

   E. $375.00

3. As an officer in a canine unit, you work primarily with a German shepherd who eats 32 ounces of dog food a day. You want to purchase enough dog food for the entire month. Each can of dog food contains 8 ounces. How many cans of dog food do you need to feed the German shepherd for a 31-day month?

   A. 35

   B. 71

   C. 124

   D. 150

   E. 416

4. You are a public employment mediator. Last week, you mediated 14 disputes, and this week you mediated another 12 disputes. During the last two weeks, you resolved 13 of the disputes you mediated. You are creating a schedule for the upcoming week and need to know how many old disputes still need mediation. How many unresolved disputes are left from the past two weeks?

   A. 10

   B. 13

   C. 17

   D. 19

   E. 23

5. You are a fire safety inspector. Yesterday you inspected an apartment building that violated five safety regulations. Each regulation violation cost the building owner $130. In addition, there is a $50 processing fine. How much did you fine the building owner?

   A. $700

   B. $735

   C. $750

   D. $815

   E. $869

6. You are a correctional supervisor. You need to order new uniforms for the correctional officers in your division. Each uniform costs $115, and you need 27 uniforms. In addition, there is a $40 shipping fee. How much do you spend on uniforms?

   A. $3,105

   B. $3,145

   C. $3,240

   D. $3,355

   E. $4,185

7. As a legal assistant working for a large law firm, one of your duties is maintaining the law firm's legal library. You need to purchase 20 state law volumes whose average cost is $400 per book and 15 federal law volumes whose average cost is $580 each. These are the only books you need to purchase. What is the total cost of ordering all necessary volumes?

   A. $14,800

   B. $15,200

   C. $16,700

   D. $17,600

   E. $20,300

8. You are a police dispatcher working for the Dallas Police Department. Today you worked 7 hours. For the first six hours, you dispatched an average of 12 police vehicles per hour. In the last hour, you dispatched 15 police vehicles. At the end of the day you have to fill out a form which asks for the total number of vehicles dispatched. How many police vehicles did you dispatch today?

   A. 72

   B. 84

   C. 87

   D. 95

   E. 105

ANSWER KEY

Item 1: **C** 23 + 15 − 21 = 17

Item 2: **D** 10 ÷ 2.5 = 4; 75 × 4 = $300

Item 3: **C** 32 ÷ 8 = 4; 4 × 31 = 124

Item 4: **B** 14 + 12 − 13 = 13

Item 5: **A** (130 × 5) + 50 = $700

Item 6: **B** (115 × 27) + 40 = $3,145

Item 7: **C** (15 × 580) + (20 × 400) = $16,700

Item 8: **C** (12 × 6) + 15 = 87

SOLVE PROBLEMS IN GEOMETRY

Perform Basic
Arithmetic
Calculations
to Solve
Workplace
Problems

**Apply
Computations
to Solve
Workplace
Problems**

Solve
Measurement
Problems

Make Spending
Decisions
to Solve
Workplace
Problems

Knowing how to determine the perimeters and areas of objects and spaces, from patrol areas to prison yards, is an important skill in the law, public safety, corrections, and security industry. It is important to be able to find the perimeter and area of both circles and rectangles.

1. You are a jail administrator. The prison that you work for is surrounded by a barbed wire fence. The fence forms a rectangle that is 100 yards wide and 150 yards long. You wish to have guards around the perimeter of the fence distanced 100 yards apart. How many guards will be guarding the perimeter of the fence?

   A. 5

   B. 7

   C. 8

   D. 10

   E. 12

2. You are a ski patrol officer. Today, you are patrolling a rectangular region that is 3.12 miles long and 2.86 miles wide. What is the area of the region you are patrolling?

   A. 6.74 square miles

   B. 8.92 square miles

   C. 9.68 square miles

   D. 10.82 square miles

   E. 12.24 square miles

3. You are a firefighter. Today you extinguished a fire in a mansion. After you extinguished the fire, you had to fill out several forms. One of the forms asks for various specifications of the location of the fire. The fire occurred a cylindrical room whose radius was 20 feet. The room was 30 feet tall. What is the volume of the cylindrical room?

   A. 6,156 cubic feet

   B. 12,884 cubic feet

   C. 21,138 cubic feet

   D. 37,680 cubic feet

   E. 41,257 cubic feet

4. You are an ambulance driver working at a hospital in a small town. You are trying to figure out the fastest way to travel from the northern side of town to the southern side. In the middle of town, there is a traffic circle with a radius of 130 feet. Knowing how far you have to drive to go around the traffic circle will allow you to effectively estimate how long it will take to drive around the traffic circle. What is the circumference of the traffic circle?

   A. 408.2 feet

   B. 810.5 feet

   C. 816.4 feet

   D. 842 feet

   E. 2,066 feet

5. You are a gaming surveillance officer. A large rectangular region of land has recently been declared a hunting-free zone. The region is 200 miles long and 130 miles wide. You have to help rewrite various hunting regulations pamphlets that will have specifications about the new hunting-free zone, including the region's area. What is the area of the region?

    A. 24,000 square miles

    B. 24,800 square miles

    C. 25,500 square miles

    D. 26,000 square miles

    E. 28,200 square miles

6. You are a parking control specialist. The town you work for has a large municipal parking lot, and you regularly check to make sure no cars are parked illegally in this lot. To determine how long it will take you to check the lot, you wish to know the perimeter and the area of the lots. The lot is a square whose sides are 500 feet long. What is the perimeter of the parking lot?

    A. 1,000 feet

    B. 1,200 feet

    C. 1,550 feet

    D. 1,750 feet

    E. 2,000 feet

7. You are a crime scene investigator. You are investigating the theft of a precious jewel from a museum. The jewel was displayed on a round table, and you need to test for fingerprints on the table. To test for fingerprints, you have to apply fingerprint powder to the surface of the table. The amount of fingerprint powder that has to be used is dependent on the area of the surface. The table has a radius of 4 feet. What is the area of the table?

    A. 12.56 square feet

    B. 25.12 square feet

    C. 50.24 square feet

    D. 57.82 square feet

    E. 58.12 square feet

8. You are a fire investigator. There was a fire in a large apartment building and you are investigating the cause of the fire. The fire affected the entire lobby of the apartment building. The lobby is a rectangular room with a width of 70 feet and a length of 130 feet. You wish to know the area of the fire to help assess the value of the damage that the fire causes. What is the area of the lobby?

    A. 9,100 square feet

    B. 9,250 square feet

    C. 9,500 square feet

    D. 10,000 square feet

    E. 10,250 square feet

ANSWER KEY

Item 1: **A** $2 \times (100 + 150) = 500$; $500 \div 100 = 5$

Item 2: **B** $3.12 \times 2.86 = 8.9232$; rounded down to 8.92 square miles

Item 3: **D** $3.14 \times 20^2 \times 30 = 37,680$ cubic feet

Item 4: **C** $130 \times 2 = 260$; $3.14 \times 260 = 816.4$ feet

Item 5: **D** $200 \times 130 = 26,000$ square miles

Item 6: **E** $4 \times 500 = 2,000$ feet

Item 7: **C** $3.14 \times 4^2 = 50.24$ square feet

Item 8: **A** $130 \times 70 = 9,100$ square feet

CALCULATE WITH CONVERSIONS AND FORMULAS

Some calculations in the law, public safety, corrections, and security industry may require using conversions and formulas. A security management specialist for an international business may need to convert currencies to calculate the cost of equipment and personnel in different countries, for example.

1. During your day as a parking enforcement officer, you come across a pair of tourists trying to figure out how much money to put into the parking meter. The meter allocates 30 minutes for each quarter deposited. How much money do the tourists need to deposit into the meter to stay for a 2-hour lunch?

   A. $0.25

   B. $0.50

   C. $1.00

   D. $1.50

   E. $2.00

2. You are a computer forensics specialist analyzing two pieces of computer equipment for a recent case. The first is a 4-gigabyte USB flash drive, valued at $9.50. The second is a 500-gigabyte external hard drive, which has value of $68.75 What is the total value of the two pieces of equipment?

   A. $73.45

   B. $75.90

   C. $77.20

   D. $78.25

   E. $80.75

3. You are the chief of police in a small town. Today you spent 5 hours, 10 minutes patrolling and 2 hours, 55 minutes doing paperwork. To fill out your time sheet, you need to know exactly how long you worked today. How much time did you spend patrolling and doing paperwork?

   A. 7 hours, 5 minutes

   B. 7 hours, 25 minutes

   C. 8 hours

   D. 8 hours, 5 minutes

   E. 8 hours, 10 minutes

4. You are an emergency preparedness program specialist helping to design an emergency plan for extreme snow storms. Last year, Colorado had two snow storms two days apart. There was 1 foot and 4 inches of snowfall during the first snow storm and 18 inches during the second storm. How much snow fell during the two snow storms?

   A. 2 feet, 7 inches

   B. 2 feet, 10 inches

   C. 3 feet

   D. 3 feet, 7 inches

   E. 4 feet

5. You are a court clerk. Today, you spent 3 hours and 20 minutes recording witness testimonies. You also spent 2.5 hours filling out forms. At the end of the day you have to fill out a time card that asks for the total amount you have worked during the day. Assuming this is the only work you did, how long did you work today?

A. 2 hours, 30 minutes
B. 3 hours, 20 minutes
C. 5 hours, 20 minutes
D. 5 hours, 30 minutes
E. 5 hours, 50 minutes

6. During a typical week as a firefighter, you work 48 hours. Each of your shifts is 8 hours long, and during each shift the firehouse receives three calls. On Monday there were 2 fires that you had to put out and on Thursday you put out 3 fires. On average, how many fires did you put out per shift?

A. 0.166
B. 0.66
C. 0.8
D. 0.833
E. 1.2

7. You are a principal law clerk. Today you have to review seven appeals. It takes half an hour to review each appeal. Of the seven appeals, you recommend that three be dismissed. You have a meeting 5 hours after you start reviewing the appeals and you want to ensure that you will have enough time before the meeting to prepare. How much time do you have to prepare for the meeting?

A. 1 hours, 30 minutes
B. 2 hours
C. 2 hours, 15 minutes
D. 2 hours, 30 minutes
E. 2 hours, 50 minutes

8. You are an animal park code enforcement officer. The park you work for prohibits dogs. If visitors bring a dog, they are given a ticket for $50. On Friday, you wrote 4 tickets; on Saturday, you wrote 2 tickets; and on Sunday, you wrote 5 tickets. Your supervisor is considering hiring another code enforcement officer and wants to know the number of tickets you typically write from Friday through Sunday. What is the average number of tickets written during this time?

A. 1.66
B. 3
C. 3.33
D. 3.66
E. 4.33

ANSWER KEY

Item 1: **C** 4 × 0.25 = $1.00
Item 2: **D** $9.50 + $68.75 = $78.25
Item 3: **D** 5 hours, 10 minutes + 2 hours, 55 minutes = 8 hours, 5 minutes
Item 4: **B** 1 foot, 4 inches = 16 inches; 16 + 18 = 34 = 2 feet 10 inches
Item 5: **E** 2.5 hours = 2 hours, 30 minutes; 3 hours, 20 minutes + 2 hours, 30 minutes = 5 hours, 50 minutes
Item 6: **D** 48 ÷ 8 = 6; 2 + 3 = 5; 5 ÷ 6 = 0.833
Item 7: **A** $\frac{1}{2} \times 7 = 3\frac{1}{2}$; $5 - 3\frac{1}{2} = 1\frac{1}{2}$; $1\frac{1}{2}$ hours = 1 hour, 30 minutes
Item 8: **D** 4 + 2 + 5 = 11; 11 ÷ 3 = 3.66

MANIPULATE FORMULAS TO SOLVE PROBLEMS

For some calculations in the law, public safety, corrections, and security industry, a formula may need to be manipulated to solve a problem. For example, a fire inspector may need to manipulate formulas to determine what caused a fire and how it spread. Workers should be able to work with basic formulas find the information required.

1. You are a forest fire investigator who is investigating a forest fire that is believed to have been ignited by unnatural causes. You have been instructed to close off a rectangular region whose area is 1.33 square miles and whose width is 0.33 miles. You need to ensure that you have enough police tape to close off the entire region. What is the perimeter of the region?

   A. 4.33 miles

   B. 8.72 miles

   C. 11.11 miles

   D. 12 miles

   E. 12.78 miles

2. You are a IT specialist in charge of maintaining computer systems in police stations. Today you need to install high-speed Internet at a police station. This requires you to run an Ethernet cables around the perimeter of the floor. The floor is rectangular, has an area of 157,080 square feet and is 231 feet wide. What is the perimeter of the floor?

   A. 462 feet

   B. 882 feet

   C. 911 feet

   D. 1,051 feet

   E. 1,822 feet

3. You are a park ranger working for a national park. Today, you have to patrol the perimeter of a large region of land to make sure there are no hunters. The region is rectangular and has an area of 6.2 square miles and a length of 3.6 miles. You need to know the perimeter of the region to figure out how much gas will be used when driving around the region. What is the perimeter of the region?

   A. 5.322 miles

   B. 6.5 miles

   C. 10.644 miles

   D. 11.732 miles

   E. 17.25 miles

4. You are a gaming surveillance deputy patrolling the shore of a circular island. A colleague's truck has broken down and you have to drive across the diameter of the island to help her. The perimeter of the island is 14.13 miles around. You need to know the diameter of the island, so you can let your colleague know approximately how long it will take to help her. What is the diameter of the island?

   A. 3.9 miles

   B. 4.2 miles

   C. 4.5 miles

   D. 4.7 miles

   E. 4.9 miles

5. You are a fire inspector. The number of fire escapes a building is required to have is determined by the dimensions of the building. You are inspecting a rectangular building whose volume is 500,000 cubic feet. The base of the building is 50 feet by 100 feet. How tall is the building?

   A. 75 feet

   B. 80 feet

   C. 95 feet

   D. 100 feet

   E. 125 feet

6. You are a crossing guard working at a traffic circle in a large city. It is your duty to ensure that people who are commuting to work can safely cross the street during rush hour. The circumference of the traffic circle is 628 feet. What is the diameter of the traffic circle?

   A. 200 feet

   B. 225 feet

   C. 235 feet

   D. 245 feet

   E. 250 feet

7. You are a crime scene analyst. A crime has occurred in a park, and you need to close off a circular region with police tape so the crime scene can be properly analyzed. The area of the region that needs to be closed off is 28.26 square feet. How many feet of police tape do you have to use?

   A. 14.22 feet

   B. 16.54 feet

   C. 16.89 feet

   D. 17.94 feet

   E. 18.84 feet

8. As an aquatics director at a public park, you have to find a new pool cleaning company to clean the diving pool. Before companies can give you an estimate, they need to know the exact dimensions of the pool. The park's diving pool is 8 feet deep. The volume of the pool is 6,400 cubic feet and the length of the pool is 40 feet. How wide is the pool?

   A. 15 feet

   B. 20 feet

   C. 25 feet

   D. 35 feet

   E. 40 feet

ANSWER KEY

Item 1:   **B** $1.33 \div 0.33 = 4.03$; $(4.03 + 0.33) \times 2 = 8.72$ miles

Item 2:   **E** $157,080 \div 231 = 680$; $2 \times (231 + 680) = 1,822$ feet

Item 3:   **C** $6.5 \div 3.6 = 1.722$; $2 \times (3.6 + 1.722) = 10.644$ miles

Item 4:   **C** $14.13 \div 3.14 = 4.5$ miles

Item 5:   **D** $50 \times 100 = 5,000$; $500,000 \div 5,000 = 100$ feet

Item 6:   **A** $628 \div 3.14 = 200$ feet

Item 7:   **E** $28.26 \div 3.14 = 9$; $\sqrt{9} = 3$; $2 \times 3 = 6$; $6 \times 3.14 = 18.84$ feet

Item 8:   **B** $8 \times 40 = 320$; $6,400 \div 320 = 20$ feet

CALCULATE COSTS AND DISCOUNTS

Perform Basic
Arithmetic
Calculations
to Solve
Workplace
Problems

Apply
Computations
to Solve
Workplace
Problems

Solve
Measurement
Problems

**Make
Spending
Decisions
to Solve
Workplace
Problems**

Many jobs in the law, public safety, corrections, and security industry require workers to calculate costs and discounts. An administrative assistant at a law firm, for example, may need to decide which office supply company to use based on the prices of the supplies and the discount offered.

1. You are a private detective. Your standard rate is $50 per hour for your services. This month you are offering 20 percent off the first three hours when a client requires more than 10 hours of your services. How much do you charge for 20 hours of work?

   A. $850

   B. $863

   C. $890

   D. $925

   E. $970

2. You are a law enforcement teacher. In addition to teaching classes, you also travel to students' houses for private tutoring. Your standard rate is $40 for one hour of tutoring. However, due to increasing gas prices you plan to increase your rate by 7%. How much do you charge for 10 hours of tutoring at your new rate?

   A. $320

   B. $372

   C. $428

   D. $452

   E. $477

3. You are a customs officer working at an international airport. A traveler is caught bringing food into the country from overseas and is fined $800. If the traveler fails to pay the fine within two months, the fine increases by 25 percent. How much does the traveler have to pay if he fails to pay the fine within the first two months?

   A. $825

   B. $900

   C. $955

   D. $1,000

   E. $1,025

4. You are an intelligence analyst. A new voice recognition program has just been released that is vastly superior to the current voice recognition software your agency is using. The software costs $800 for the basic program and an additional $100 for technical support. Also, the company will take 13 percent off of the cost of the software if you purchase the technical support. How much does the program and the technical support cost?

   A. $744

   B. $796

   C. $859

   D. $883

   E. $900

5. You are a secretary working for a law firm in Chicago. The law firm you work for has just been hired by a client in Seattle. You have to book seven plane tickets from Chicago to Seattle. Each round trip plane ticket costs $300 from the airline. However, you found a travel agent who is able to offer you a 50 percent discount on two of the tickets. How much do the plane tickets cost?

A. $1,700

B. $1,775

C. $1,800

D. $1,955

E. $1,985

6. You are a ski patrol director. You need to purchase six new snowmobiles for your ski patrol officers. The company you are purchasing the snowmobiles from offers an 8 percent discount on all orders greater than $6,000. The company sells snowmobiles for $2,500 each. How much do you spend on snowmobiles?

A. $13,800

B. $14,000

C. $14,650

D. $15,530

E. $17,200

7. You are a supply officer working in a federal prison. You need to purchase new mattresses for the prison cells. There are 150 prison cells and each cell needs two new mattresses. The retailer you are buying from sells one mattress for $60. The retailer also decides to give you 50 percent off 50 of the mattresses, since you are buying in bulk. How much do you spend on mattresses?

A. $14,285

B. $14,980

C. $15,500

D. $16,500

E. $17,000

8. You are a sheriff. The canine officers have requested new leashes for their dogs. You decide to purchase 25 leather leashes. The animal supply store sells leather leashes for $10 each and charges 15% for shipping. How much do you spend on the leashes?

A. $212.50

B. $287.50

C. $300.00

D. $355.50

E. $375.00

ANSWER KEY

Item 1: **E** 17 × 50 = 850; 3 × 50 = 150; 150 − (0.20 × 150) = 120; 120 + 850 = $970

Item 2: **C** 40 + (40 × 0.07) = 42.80; 42.80 × 10 = $428

Item 3: **D** 800 × 25% = 200; 800 + 200 = $1,000

Item 4: **B** 13% × 800 = 104; 800 − 104 + 100 = $796

Item 5: **C** 300 × 5 = 1,500; 300 × 2 = 600; 600 − (0.50 × 600) = 300; 1,500 + 300 = $1,800

Item 6: **A** 6 × 2,500 = 15,000; 15,000 − (0.08 × 15,000) = $13,800

Item 7: **D** 60 × 250 = 15,000; 60 × 50 = 3,000; 3,000 − (0.50 × 3,000) = 1,500; 1,500 + 15,000 = $16,500

Item 8: **B** 25 × 10 = 250; 250 + (0.15 × 250) = $287.50

MAKE CONSUMER COMPARISONS

Law, public safety, corrections, and security workers who make purchasing decisions or recommendations must often make calculations that compare two or more purchasing options. A sheriff may need to compare the cost of several mobile devices before purchasing them for deputies. Being able to make these calculations and find the best deal is an important industry skill.

1. As an administrative assistant working at a large law firm, you need to purchase 1,000 legal pads for your law firm. Office Supplier A sells boxes of 50 legal pads for $15 each and offers 15 percent off purchases over $500. Office Supplier B sells boxes of 100 legal pads for $32 each and offers a 10 percent discount for orders over $300. What is the minimum you can spend on legal pads?

   A. $288

   B. $300

   C. $315

   D. $320

   E. $350

2. You are a latent fingerprint examiner. When examining objects containing fingerprints, you need to wear rubber gloves to prevent destruction of the prints. You need to purchase 1,500 disposable rubber gloves. Supplier A sells boxes of 75 gloves costing $9 per box. Supplier B sells boxes of 25 gloves costing $4 per box. How much will you save by going with the supplier with the best deal?

   A. $60

   B. $180

   C. $240

   D. $300

   E. $420

3. You are a security director working for an office building. You need to purchase 16 security cameras. Supplier A charges $130 for each security camera and a flat rate of $400 for installation. Supplier B charges $200 per camera and provides free installation. What is the minimum you can spend on security cameras and installation?

   A. $2,100

   B. $2,480

   C. $2,670

   D. $3,200

   E. $3,455

4. You are a firefighter teaching a class on forest fire prevention. You want to purchase 2,000 colored fliers to advertise this class. Printer A charges $10 for a box of 100 colored fliers. Printer B charges $7 for a box of 75 black and white fliers, with an additional $2 per box if you want colored fliers. What is the minimum you can spend on fliers?

   A. $54

   B. $189

   C. $200

   D. $243

   E. $443

5. You are a water safety instructor teaching a swimming class for elementary school children. You need to purchase 40 life jackets for the class. One supplier sells life jackets for $40.20 each and offers free shipping. Another supplier sells life jackets for $39 each and charges $47.50 for shipping. What is the minimum you can spend on life jackets?

A. $1,526.50

B. $1,538.00

C. $1,550.00

D. $1,607.50

E. $1,608.00

6. You are a forensic science lab technician. You need to purchase a new blood analysis machine. One medical supply retail store sells the machine you need for $3,500 and offers a 15 percent discount for first-time customers. A second medical supply retail store sells the machine you need for $3,700 and offers a $400 discount for first-time customers. What is the least you can spend on a blood analysis machine?

A. $2,450

B. $2,625

C. $2,800

D. $2,975

E. $3,300

7. You are a justice teaching assistant. You need to purchase 30 subscriptions to an online testing service. Company A offers a one-year subscription for $60 a student, offers a $300 discount on orders over $2,000. At Company B, they offer a subscription to their website for $55 a year per student. There is also a flat $80 fee per school. What is the least amount of money you can spend on the 30 subscriptions?

A. $1,700

B. $1,730

C. $1,780

D. $1,800

E. $1,850

8. You are judicial law clerk. The case you are working on requires a witness to be interviewed. You have to arrange for a witness to be brought to the courthouse by a taxi service. The drive from the witness's house to the courthouse is 15.2 miles. Taxi Service A charges $3.50 a mile in addition to a flat charge of $5. Taxi Service B charges $4.25 a mile. What is the least amount of money you can spend on the taxi service?

A. $52.00

B. $54.35

C. $58.20

D. $64.60

E. $67.80

ANSWER KEY

Item 1: **A** Supplier A: 1,000 ÷ 50 = 20; 20 × 15 = $300; Supplier B: 1,000 ÷ 100 = 10; 10 × 32 = 320; 320 × 0.10 = 32; 320 − 32 = $288

Item 2: **A** Supplier A: 1,500 ÷ 75 = 20; 20 × 9 = $180; Supplier B: 1,500 ÷ 25 = 60; 60 × 4 = $240; 240 − 180 = $60

Item 3: **B** Supplier A: 130 × 16 = 2,080; 2,080 + 400 = $2,480; Supplier B: 200 × 16 = $3,200

Item 4: **C** Printer A: 2,000 ÷ 100 = 20; 20 × 10 = $200; Printer B: 2,000 ÷ 75 = 26.67; 27 × 7 = 189; 27 × 2 = 54; 189 + 54 = $243

Item 5: **D** Supplier 1: 40.20 × 40 = $1,608; Supplier 2: 39 × 40 + 47.50 = $1,607.50

Item 6: **D** Store 1: 3,500 − (0.15 × 3,500) = $2,975; Store 2: 3,700 − 400 = $3,300

Item 7: **B** Company A: 60 × 30 = $1,800; Company B: 55 × 30 + 80 = $1,730

Item 8: **C** Taxi Service A: 3.50 × 15.2 + 5.00 = $58.20; Taxi Service B: 4.25 × 15.2 = $64.60

CAREER CLUSTERS AND PATHWAYS

A **career cluster** is a grouping of jobs and industries based on common characteristics. A **career pathway** is an area of focus within a career cluster. You can explore each of the following career clusters and pathways in McGraw-Hill Workforce's *Career Companion* series.

Agriculture, Food & Natural Resources
Food Products and Processing Systems
Plant Systems
Animal Systems
Power, Structural & Technical Systems
Natural Resources Systems
Environmental Service Systems
Agribusiness Systems

Architecture & Construction
Design/Pre-Construction
Construction
Maintenance/Operations

Arts, Audio/Video Technology & Communications
Audio and Video Technology and Film
Printing Technology
Visual Arts
Performing Arts
Journalism and Broadcasting
Telecommunications

Business Management & Administration
General Management
Business Information Management
Human Resources Management
Operations Management
Administrative Support

Education & Training
Administration and Administrative Support
Professional Support Services
Teaching/Training

Finance
Securities & Investments
Business Finance
Accounting
Insurance
Banking Services

Government & Public Administration
Governance
National Security
Foreign Service
Planning
Revenue and Taxation
Regulation
Public Management and Administration

Health Science
Therapeutic Services
Diagnostic Services
Health Informatics
Support Services
Biotechnology Research and Development

Hospitality & Tourism
Restaurants and Food/Beverage Services
Lodging
Travel & Tourism
Recreation, Amusements & Attractions

Human Services
Early Childhood Development & Services
Counseling & Mental Health Services
Family & Community Services
Personal Care Services
Consumer Services

Information Technology
Network Systems
Information Support and Services
Web and Digital Communications
Programming and Software Development

Law, Public Safety, Corrections & Security
Correction Services
Emergency and Fire Management Services
Security & Protective Services
Law Enforcement Services
Legal Services

Manufacturing
Production
Manufacturing Production Process Development
Maintenance, Installation & Repair
Quality Assurance
Logistics & Inventory Control
Health, Safety and Environmental Assurance

Marketing
Marketing Management
Professional Sales
Merchandising
Marketing Communications
Marketing Research

Science, Technology, Engineering & Mathematics
Engineering and Technology
Science and Math

Transportation, Distribution & Logistics
Transportation Operations
Logistics Planning and Management Services
Warehousing and Distribution Center Operations
Facility and Mobile Equipment Maintenance
Transportation Systems/Infrastructure Planning, Management and Regulation
Health, Safety and Environmental Management
Sales and Service